Praise for *True Tales from the Campaign Trail*

Every campaign is nothing more than a story, a snapshot of our time. And the best storytellers are the people who work on the campaigns. The tales in this book will touch your heart and make you laugh out loud.

—**Nan Whaley, mayor of Dayton, Ohio**

Jerry Austin teaches American politics. His text is composed of tales from the field—he lives, collects, and publishes them, his own and those of some of America's foremost practitioners of political arts and sciences. Austin leads us in learning from them. Or just grabbing a favorite beverage and enjoying the hell out of them both. Either way these are great stories and this is a terrific read and you'll learn more about politics than you ever got from any poli-sci course. Because Jerry Austin is one super teacher.

—**Tom Sawyer (congressman, state senator, mayor of Akron and state representative)**

Bliss Institute Series

John C. Green, Editor

Jerry Austin, *True Tales from the Campaign Trail, Vol. 2: Stories Only Political Consultants Can Tell*

William Hershey and Colleagues, *Profiles in Achievement: The Gifts, Quirks and Foibles of Ohio's Best Politicians*

Joy Marsella, *Creating a New Civility*

William Hershey, *Quick & Quotable: Columns from Washington, 1985–1997*

Jerry Austin, *True Tales from the Campaign Trail: Stories Only Political Consultants Can Tell*

Christopher J. Galdieri, Tauna S. Sisco, and Jennifer C. Lucas, editors, *Races, Reforms, & Policy: Implications of the 2014 Midterm Elections*

Tauna S. Sisco, Jennifer C. Lucas, and Christopher J. Galdieri, editors, *Political Communication & Strategy: Consequences of the 2014 Midterm Elections*

William L. Hershey and John C. Green, *Mr. Chairman: The Life and Times of Ray C. Bliss*

Douglas M. Brattebo, Tom Lansford, Jack Covarrubias, and Robert J. Pauly Jr., editors, *Culture, Rhetoric, and Voting: The Presidential Election of 2012*

Douglas M. Brattebo, Tom Lansford, and Jack Covarrubias, editors, *A Transformation in American National Politics: The Presidential Election of 2012*

Daniel J. Coffey, John C. Green, David B. Cohen, and Stephen C. Brooks, *Buckeye Battleground: Ohio, Campaigns, and Elections in the Twenty-First Century*

Lee Leonard, *A Columnist's View of Capitol Square: Ohio Politics and Government, 1969–2005*

Abe Zaidan, with John C. Green, *Portraits of Power: Ohio and National Politics, 1964–2000*

True Tales from the Campaign Trail
Stories Only Political Consultants Can Tell

Volume 2

Written and compiled by Jerry Austin

University of Akron Press
Akron, Ohio

All inquiries and permission requests should be addressed to the Publisher, The University of Akron Press, Akron, Ohio 44325-1703.

ISBN: 978-1-62922-017-8 (paper)
ISBN: 978-1-62922-045-1 (ePDF)
ISBN: 978-1-62922-021-5 (ePub)

A catalog record for this title is available from the Library of Congress.

∞ The paper used in this publication meets the minimum requirements of ANSI/NISO z39.48–1992 (Permanence of Paper).

Cover design and illustration: Doug Granger

True Tales from the Campaign Trail was designed and typeset in Adobe Caslon with Futura display by Beth Pratt. *True Tales from the Campaign Trail* was printed on sixty-pound white and bound by Bookmasters of Ashland, Ohio.

Contents

II. Campaigns

III. Beginnings and Endings

IV. Politics

Introduction

There I was in Monrovia, Liberia in October of 2019, helping train seventy-five young African leaders from ten countries in West Africa.

I was the guest speaker for days three and four of a five-day training session under the auspices of Young Political Leaders Africa. My topics were "How to Run a Campaign" and "What Are the Attributes of a Good Candidate?"

After I was introduced, I asked each participant to stand up and introduce themselves to the group. I reminded them of the importance of a good candidate having the ability to communicate and speaking was the main vehicle for communicating.

The first speaker, a young woman from Ghana stated, "I don't know what to say."

I replied, "Tell me about yourself as if you were telling me a story."

For the next day and a half, the seventy-five participants told me and their colleagues their story.

The next exercise was to tell a story about either someone else or about an incident they experienced. This activity captured the next day and a half.

Story telling is what *True Tales from the Campaign Trail, Volume 2*, is about. But story telling is also a campaign tool.

As a postscript to the Liberia conference, I received an email a few months later. It was from my first speaker from Ghana. I did not know she was in the middle of a campaign for their version of state representative. She had run four years ago and lost. She was the first female to compete for an office in her area of Ghana.

Her email thanked me for teaching her to tell stories as a campaign strategy. She won her race. Effective story telling was the difference.

Volume 2 contains stories not as triumphant as my friend from Ghana, but they do continue the behind-the-curtain look at campaigns from the great political consultant story tellers of the last forty years begun with Volume 1.* These stories are from both Democrats and Republicans. They share a love of politics/campaigns and the people they've met during their careers.

I would like to thank my fellow consultants who shared their stories, and Doug Granger who designed the covers for Volumes 1 and 2. A special thanks to the staff of the Ray C. Bliss Institute of Applied Politics at The University Akron, and Director Dr. John C. Green, whose editing and encouragement made both volumes possible.

ENJOY!
Gerald "Jerry" Austin
Tallmadge, Ohio
Summer 2020

---

* Gerald Austin, *True Tales from the Campaign Trail.* Akron, Ohio, University of Akron Press, 2017.

I. Strother Stories

Dedication

Raymond Strother is to political consulting what Babe Ruth was to baseball, Red Grange was to football, and Red Auerbach was to basketball. He put the profession on the map.

Ray has been a mentor and friend to most of the storytellers in this book.

This paragraph promoting Ray's book, *Falling Up: How A Redneck Helped Invent Political Consulting,*[*] best describes him:

> *Beneath the white hot-glare of modern media-sphere, where "old pol," shake every-hand-campaigns have given way to electronic image making and speed-of-light smear tactics, Ray Strother rolls cheerily along. A cross between a patriotic redneck raconteur and a TV-savvy renaissance man, Strother is unafraid to name names and refuses to mince words in tales of what he calls "the beauty and gore" of American politics.*

Thank you, Ray!

---

[*] Raymond Strother, *Falling Up: How a Redneck Helped Invent Political Consulting.* Baton Rouge: LSU Press, 2005.

Sound Problem

Raymond Strother

When I was a press secretary, I took myself very seriously. I was twenty-three or twenty-four years old. I would write long speeches for Louisiana Governor John McKeithen and he would read them and say, "Good speech, good speech," fold them and put it in his pocket. When he'd get up on the podium, he'd take the speech out, put it down and say, "I have a speech, but I have a message on my heart." And he'd dramatically throw my speech away.

So, as I told Jerry Austin, "I have a message on my heart." And I was thinking about our business, political consulting. If life was a bag and you wanted to fill it with great stories, you'd have to become a political consultant. Because in consulting you have humor, terror, blackness, light, laughs, and every human emotion. Soon your bag would be overflowing. I had so many stories that I actually ended up writing a book about them, *Falling Up,* and I know, Jerry, you've done the same thing.

So, I was thinking this morning: So, how does one begin? My beginning would be Louisiana. Funny things happen. And, as a consultant, one must make constant adjustments, be quick on one's feet, and have a golden tongue.

---

*Strother, *Falling Up*. Material also found in this book appears in some of the following stories, retold by the author and identified in footnotes. It is included here with permission from the Louisiana State University Press.

I was filming a five-minute television commercial for a candidate for governor. He was a good-looking guy with an attractive wife. I loved five-minute pieces, and at that time, they were easy to buy at the end of the ten p.m. news.

In this mini-documentary about the happy candidate and his family, we had gone out to a pretty lake with a grassy bank surrounded by moss-hung oak trees. About fifty yards from the lake was a knoll, maybe fifty or sixty feet higher than the bank of the lake. So, I put a thirty-five-millimeter camera, my soundman, and all our equipment on the knoll. It was the perfect, warm scene. He was holding hands with his wife walking by the lake. Most of my work at the time was *cinema verité* ("truthful cinema") and I was always searching for an unguarded moment that would sound authentic to the viewer.

The soundman, Harry Lapham, earlier in the day, had miked the couple for another scene. I had the sound man record so I might pick up a moment of sound that could be used. This could also alert the camera man, Bob Fiori, if they announced any change in their walk. All of the crew could hear the candidate and his wife through a small speaker in the recorder. I stood on the knoll and gave directions through a bullhorn.

Unfortunately, the happy couple had forgotten they were miked, and we had neglected to tell them their mikes were hot. All consultants have a story about a client having an unguarded private conversation or going into a toilet with a hot mike.

This candidate, a true ham, had his arm around his wife and they were holding hands—anything he thought would prove him to be a good husband. They were making casual conversation.

"Where were you last night?" he asked.

"Where do you think I was? I was doing the same thing you were doing. I was f**king your press secretary, just like you f**cked (name omitted.)"

All of the crew looked at me in horror. The soundman shrugged his shoulders. The lighting director was laughing into his hands. One of the grips had fallen to his knees and was pounding the ground.

About that time the happy couple realized they were wearing hot mikes and looked up the hill at us. It was a frozen moment in time.

I grabbed my bullhorn, "I'm sorry, but you have to start again. We have a problem with our sound; we can't hear anything. Go back to where you started."

I had made the adjustment to not embarrass him or her, and we went on with our filming like nothing had ever happened.

This story has always pleased me. The candidate lost. He deserved to.

That Cadillac Don't Run on Water
Raymond Strother

One of my first campaigns gave me a humorous story I have since told many times. I was just out of graduate school and had been hired to conduct a congressional campaign. Decades ago, the African American vote was controlled by a handful of leaders. They did the turnout and knocked on doors, handed out sample ballots, and usually had a small army of paid "volunteers" to do the tasks. Many of the "leaders" were preachers. They would come to the campaign office with bills for the services of their army.

There was a very popular Black preacher in one section of the state named Reverend Florida. We could afford only so many armies, so he was not one of our team. But one day he drove up to campaign headquarters and came in. He was a three-hundred-pound man in a preacher suit and tie. He wore a heavy gold cross around his neck.

"Uh-oh," I said to myself, "we're gonna be shaken down for some money."

We didn't have money. Had the campaign had money they would have hired a better-known consultant than me.

He came in and said, "Boys, I want to tell you. I love your candidate. I've been campaigning for him all over the district; I've been on the highways, and interstates, the gravel roads, the bi-ways, and the trails. I've been all over. I've been in the dives; I've been in the good restaurants; I've been everywhere campaigning for your man."

I nodded, expecting the punch line, and he said, "And I don't want anything. I don't want any money."

I said, "Really?"

He said, "No, no, I don't want to be paid for doing this, because I'm doing the right thing."

I was stunned. "Well, I really appreciate that, Reverend Florida."

He said, "Now, let me tell you, I do need about $3,000 in cash today."

I said, "Reverend Florida, you said that you didn't need any money."

He said, "I don't."

But then he said, "Boy, do you think that Cadillac runs on water?"

Pointing at a big Cadillac outside, he repeated, "That Cadillac don't run on water."

I don't remember whether we paid Reverend Florida or not. The "don't run on water" line became part of my campaign vocabulary.

A Million Dollar Campaign
Raymond Strother

Louisiana stories, in my opinion, are some of the best stories because they are a combination of Latin culture and laissez-faire. I've represented almost everyone in the state at one time or another. I represented Senators Russell Long, Bennett Johnson, John Breaux and Mary Landrieu, and I represented Governors John McKeithen, Edwin Edwards and Buddy Roemer, plus a lot of congressmen, such as Gillis Long.

The most wonderful thing that happened out of all those elections is great stories.

In 1970, my firm had signed with Edwin Edwards, a congressman running for governor of Louisiana. I went to Europe with my wife, and when I got back, my partner said, "We no longer represent Congressman Edwin Edwards. We now represent Governor Jimmie Davis."

I said, "What?"

The reason was *pure* politics. Judge Edmund Reggies was the godfather of politics in Louisiana and an early Edwards supporter. But then the Reggies and Edwards families had a falling out: one of Edwards daughters blackballed one of Reggies' daughters from joining a college sorority. Reggie called my partner and said, "We're going to all go to Jimmie Davis."

Jimmie Davis was an old Louisiana governor who had been elected to the office twice before. He was a bad governor two times, in the mid-1940s and the early 1960s, because you could only serve one term at a time as Louisiana governor in those days. So, every decision was short-term and comeback attempts were common.

I was young, twenty-four or twenty-five years old. My partner didn't do a lot, he mostly laid on the couch. I traveled with the politicians, which ended up being a good thing because I learned something about politics, by osmosis, doing the work. I was going to make Davis' television, his radio, write his speeches, and be his press secretary. And I was going to make a lot of money.

So, I traveled with Jimmie Davis for a year and everything about him was a story.

But we weren't going to win. There was never any hope of that. I knew it and Davis knew it. In fact, we did lose: Davis finished fourth in the Democratic primary. In first place—and the eventually governor—was Edwin Edwards, our original client.

Knowing he couldn't win put Davis in a kind of relaxed position.

But knowing he couldn't win put me in a curious position. Why was Davis running? I found out why: he was totally corrupt.

Because he'd been governor before, people owed him big for bridges, for highways, for all kinds of things. He would go to a hotel and he'd send out word to his friends that he needed money, in cash, and they would come bring him "campaign contributions."

We were in New Orleans one time at the Roosevelt Hotel, where there's a presidential suite that all the governors use.

Davis said, "Raymond, you go down now to the bar (which had a low wall) and you watch who comes in. You know all the players and when money people come in, don't let them get to the campaign treasurer, who will be standing by the elevator because only half of their money will make it up here to me. You get to them first and bring them to the back elevator."

I said, "Yes sir."

I did that time after time. I'd take a money man up the back elevator and I would leave. They would go into the bedroom and shut the door. Then I'd see him or her leave quickly. I knew they'd made a drop-off of money.

Accidentally, I walked into the room one afternoon. The bed was stacked with hundred-dollar bills. I would guess $75,000 to $100,000 in hundred-dollar bills—not in order, just in stacks, just piles of stacks. I'd quickly backed out of the room.

Then we went out to the airport and got in our campaign plane and flew to Baton Rouge, which was only eighty-five miles away. The campaign manager was wringing his hands saying, "Raymond, Raymond, Raymond. I've got to have money for television tonight. It's time to pay the television bill. Did you collect the money?"

I said, "Yeah, we got plenty of money."

He said, "Well, okay, I'll go talk to Jimmie."

He went over to Davis and he said, "Governor, Governor, I need some money." Davis said, "Well, I don't know."

He reached in his pocket. He had a paperclip and he had about $250 in the paperclip.

Davis said, "I'll give you about half of what I've got" and gave him about $150.

We got back on the airplane, and left, with Davis keeping all the money for himself. The campaign manager had to go out and raise money from other people like himself to pay for everything.

I estimated one time that Davis had picked up well in excess of $1 million in hundred-dollar bills during the time I traveled with him.*

---

*For material related to this story see Strother, *Falling Up*, 69–71, 77–78.

Losing Papa Brock
Raymond Strother

During the 1970-71 Louisiana gubernatorial campaign, I traveled with Jimmie Davis. He was known as the "singing governor" because of his successful career as country and gospel singer. He is credited with writing the hit song "You are My Sunshine," but he had sort of stolen it. If you look at the old sheet music, his name is there, but with someone else. He paid that somebody ten dollars for it. And he made millions of dollars on it.

It was his third campaign for governor. He'd leave the governor's chair, go to Hollywood and make western movies, along with the likes of the "singing cowboys" Gene Autry and Roy Rodgers. Then he'd run for governor again.

To back up Davis' singing, the campaign had a band, a very good band, hired from around the country. It had about five people, including Eddy Reaven, who later got to be a big star in Nashville, and Davis's second wife Anna Carter Gordon Davis, who was part of Carter family singers, known as the Chuck Wagon Gang. Davis had just married her for the campaign. And he had a renowned gospel group from Nashville, the Speer Family.

We traveled around the state giving performances. I don't know if there was any politics involved with it or not, but we'd get performances. We had a trailer that the sound truck towed around. It was like a flower. The petals would open and there would be a piano, drums, electric guitars, amplifiers, and a long extension cord. All you'd have to do is go into the courthouse and plug it in, and then you'd have a rally on the courthouse steps. That's the way they did in the 1940s. That's way old-time Louisiana politicians worked.

Davis didn't know what to make of me. I was riding the bus with him and he just couldn't place me, "What do you do?" He didn't know what I did because his previous campaigns didn't have media people. I didn't write his speeches because Davis gave the same speeches as in 1944 when he was first elected governor, with no changes whatsoever. I realized right away that he didn't believe in polling, and he wouldn't do anything with the press, which he despised.

He finally decided I was in entertainment. Davis came up to me one day and said, "You're in public relations?"

I said, "Yeah, I guess."

He said, "I want to you to start traveling with the band. Those boys are showing up late to performances."

Davis wouldn't even call it a campaign; he'd call it performances because he was really just raising money.

So, he assigned me to the band, "You stay with the band and keep them out of trouble."

All country music bands are a little wild and these were fairly young guys. In fact, the Speer Family gospel group was always afraid that the band would get too friendly with the female singers. They would always lock the women up in the bus so the band members couldn't get to them.

Because I disliked Davis intensely, I was very happy to move out of the bus and travel with the band in their van.

One night we were in Opelousas and I had the band in a restaurant named Swallows. It had great Cajun seafood restaurant and everyone was about half drunk. I had been there many times before.

Then in walked one of the most notorious men in Louisiana, Sheriff Cat Doucet of St. Landry Parish. He was little man, about five foot five, wearing a foot-tall Stetson western hat that took him up over six-foot tall, along with cowboy boots and two guns slung over each hip like Matt Dillon. He was staggering drunk. He could barely walk.

Cat had some deputies with him, and he spotted me. I had known him for a while. I had been the press secretary to the outgoing governor. Cat was a political power in that part of the state. For some reason he didn't call me Strother, maybe he couldn't say it. He would call me "Stroker." He always did.

Cat came over, put his arm around me, and said, "Stroker, I'm so glad to see you. You're doing such a wonderful thing for the people of Louisiana by electing Jimmie back to governor again. That will be wonderful for the state."

Why did Cat want Jimmie elected? Because Cat had two brothels in Opelousas and a small gambling casino with a roulette wheel, cards, and blackjack. Davis would always allow gambling and prostitution. He didn't care because the owners paid him off. My former boss, Governor McKeithen, had shut down gambling and prostitution.

He said, "I just love you boys so much. The band here, I love the band. I love each of these boys like they were my son."

I said, "Well, that's good, Cat."

He said, "Boys, I've got to do something for you. I got to do something good." He reached inside his pocket and pulled out a bunch of business cards. He would look down the line, write a note, and hand me a card until he had written a note for everybody in the band and me—all six or seven of us.

He said, "You boys have a good time."

Then Cat walked, wandered, and staggered off.

I looked at the card. It had a woman holding her breast and it said, "Bet you didn't know we handle these. The Gate."

On the back, it said, "Give this boy anything he wants free—Cat."

By this time, the band was looking at the cards.

Then Eddie said, "What do you have there, Mr. Raymond?" which is a Southern way of saying things, calling somebody's name.

I said, "Well, the sheriff owns a brothel."

"A brothel?"

"A whorehouse. What I have here is a free pass to the whorehouse, Mr. Eddie."

"Oh, where is it?"

"It's about three blocks from here."

"Oh, yeah? We want to go over there and take a look."

"Boys, we got to be at our next stop tonight because we have an eight o'clock show."

"Let's just go look around."

So, we drive up to The Gate. It was surrounded by a corrugated metal fence, so you couldn't see through it. The fence was ten feet tall, painted green, and had a gate, with a big sign saying "The Gate" over it.

I went up to the gate and a deputy sheriff opened it. We drove in, parked, and walked up to the front door. There was a small desk outside the door with another deputy sheriff. He said, "Boys, I want your driver's license and your pistols. You can pick them up when you leave."

I didn't have a pistol—a couple of band members did—but anyway, we gave him our pistols and licenses and went into the house.

It was quite attractive. The madam, her name was Maggie, looked at our cards. She was very gracious and she knew who we were. We sat on these sofas and chairs, while she paraded all the girls by.

Well, the boys started drinking beer at about five dollars a piece. They would pick a girl and drift off.

I was in charge of these boys. I thought, "This isn't going to end well."

I finally told Eddie, as he was the last to go, "I'm going go back to Swallows and have a couple of scotches, and I'll come back to pick you boys up at eleven o'clock."

"Okay."

So, I went back at eleven, I got the madam to round all the boys up. I drove them back to the campaign bus, maybe fifty miles away. The next morning, they got up and did their eight o'clock show, their twelve o'clock show, and their three o'clock show.

The next night, as we're wrapping up the bass drums, closing the stage, and unplugging the wires, Eddie said, "Let's go."

I said, "Where we going?"

"We're going back to The Gate."

"Going back?"

"Yeah, the cards say, 'Give this boy anything the wants free,' and they didn't take them away from us. We think this card is still good."

"That's a hundred miles away, Eddie."

"Yeah, the band's ready to go."

Well, I argued with them a little bit, but knew I couldn't win. I didn't care anyway and drove them back to The Gate.

So, I drove them to The Gate. Every. Single. Night. Louisiana is a fairly large state. Wherever we were, be it New Orleans, be it Lake Charles, be it Shreveport, we were driving to The Gate.

So, one night, we were getting ready to go to The Gate and Papa Brock Speer comes up, the head of the Speer Family gospel group.

He said, "Raymond, where are you boys going?"

I said, "We're just going down the road, Papa Brock, you don't need to know."

"Yeah, I'm going with you."

"No, I don't think so."

"No, I want to go with you. Every night you boys go off someplace. I sit there with these women playing cards."

I was arguing with him when Eddies comes around, Eddy's just a lovable guy, and said, "Oh, let Papa go with us."

"I don't think it's a good idea, boys."

"No, Papa's going with us."

So, Papa loaded in the van with us, and we drove about a hundred and fifty miles because we were in Monroe, Louisiana—or at least that was going to be where we were the next morning at eight o'clock.

We got to The Gate, I dropped them off at the door, and I went to Swallows, had a few drinks, ate dinner, and killed time. At eleven o'clock, I went to collect all the boys. They all showed up very promptly, basically sober.

I said, "Where's Papa Brock?"

"I don't know, haven't seen him."

I turned to Maggie and said, "Where's Papa?"

She said, "Is he the preacher?"

"Yeah."

"I don't know. I saw him when you boys came in."

"We got to have Papa—he's the head of this gospel group!"

"Let's go look around."

We went door-to-door upstairs, knocked on doors, and the prostitutes would come out and say, "No, he's not here," but Maggie said go look under the bed, in the closet, in the bathroom, make sure he's not here. I think there were eight girls and went to all eight of them. But no Papa Brock.

We looked and looked and still no Papa Brock.

My watch showed it was almost two a.m. Our show was at eight a.m., and it's in Monroe, which is a hundred and fifty miles away on bad roads.

I said, "Boys, we're going to have to leave Papa Brock, we got to go. We'll barely make it."

We make it and the band got set up, just as Davis came out.

He said, "Raymond, I've heard some rumors, where's Papa Brock?"

Davis exactly knew the whole story. I think Cat called him and told him the whole story.

"Governor, I don't know. I intend to go back and look for him."

"No, you go back right now. If you don't find him, don't come back here. Just keep going and tell your partner that this arrangement's over."

So, I drive back a hundred and fifty miles to the whorehouse.

I wake up Maggie and said, "I've got to find Papa Brock."

She said, "I don't know. I can't figure it out. Could he have wandered off someplace? Go to a local bar?"

"He doesn't drink."

"The only other place I know we have is for overflow crowds. We have a couple trailers out back, and a couple of the girls stay out there. Let's go look and see if he went out there."

So, we go out of the house, into the back of the lot, and there are a couple trailers. We knocked on a door. A young lady opened the door, and there was Papa drunk, in his shorts, standing there, just weaving. He was so drunk he couldn't walk.

"Oh my God."

I get Papa Brock loaded in the van and I drive him back a hundred and fifty miles to the campaign bus.

Mrs. Speer comes out and she wants to hit me. She wants to do everything bad she can to me. Papa Brock had been dried out for about a year ago. He'd gone to an institution, dried out for being a drunk, and he'd fallen off the wagon in the whorehouse. They slammed him in the bus and took him back to Nashville, back to the institution. That was the end of the Speer Family's association with the campaign.

At that point, Davis and I were really on the outs because I had done that to Papa—anyway what he thought I had done. Davis didn't mind the boys going to The Gate; he minded the gospel group quitting the campaign.*

---

*For related material and part of this story, see Strother, *Falling Up*, 72–75, 83–83.

Please Don't Kill a Reporter
Raymond Strother

One of the hardest things about traveling with Jimmie Davis was that he wouldn't speak with reporters covering the campaign.

One night, on a lonely dark road, I'm in the campaign bus bumping around with a bunch of hillbilly guitar players.

I said, "Governor, you got to talk to the press. You got to. Look, I'm an old newspaperman. I got started with the Associated Press. You're making me a laughingstock. You got to talk to press."

"I don't."

"Yes, you do."

We argued and argued. He finally said, "Stop the bus. Stop the bus. Get out."

He threw me off the bus in the middle of nowhere.

When I got back on the bus the next morning, Davis met me and never mentioned it. But the disagreement went on.

A bit later, we were in Shreveport and Davis still refused to talk to reporters.

He said, "No, they just lie. They all want to talk about that bridge in Shreveport. They'll accuse me of having that bridge turned to go through my land. I'm not going to talk to reporters."

Well, there *was* a bridge in Shreveport that went over a river and then turned hard right—and went through his land.

So that night in Shreveport, one of my reporter friends came up to me and said, "Raymond, we're going to talk to the governor. What we're going to do is we're going to join hands around the stage, and he can't get through us."

I said, "Good luck, but I've got to tell him."

He said, "It doesn't matter if you tell him or not."

So, I went to Davis and told him what was planned.

He said, "When do you think they would do that?"

"Well, you always end your acts with singing 'You Are My Sunshine.' But tonight don't end your act that way, end it with something else, but announce early that you're going to sing 'You Are My Sunshine,' but say because the folks have been so good to me, I'm also going to play another one of your favorites, like the 'Columbus Stockade Blues' or something."

"That's a good idea."

"Then jump off the stage after you sing 'You are My Sunshine' and go lock yourself in the bus."

So, he did that. After 'You Are My Sunshine,' he put down his guitar and said, "Thank you. Now we're going to play another number because you have been so kind. Just a minute, I need to get a drink of water."

He jumped off the backstage, ran to his bus, went in the bus, and locked it. And the press chased him. When they were chasing him, he was screaming over his shoulder, "Talk to Raymond. Just talk to Raymond. Just talk to Raymond."

The reporters didn't want to talk to me. I was a kid press secretary, but anyway I'm the only target they have. So, they surround me to talk to me.

Then this big redneck guy in coveralls and a straw hat comes up. He must weigh three hundred pounds. He's mad as hell.

He yells, "You see what they just did to Governor Jimmie and chased him into his bus?"

I said, "Yeah."

He said, "I'm gonna kill these reporters. I'm gonna kill them!"

He grabbed this little reporter, a small guy, and repeated, "I'm gonna kill him."

I grabbed him and said, "Please don't kill a reporter. Please don't kill a reporter."

He said, "Mr. Raymond, can I just break a leg or something?"

Anyway, the whole incident was recorded on television, on radio, with me pleading, "Please don't kill a reporter."

The next day, the editorial cartoon in the newspaper was this big guy and me saying, "Please don't kill the reporters."*

---

*For related material and part of this story, see Strother, *Falling Up*, 79–81.

Buick and Beer
Raymond Strother

One of the interesting characters with the Jimmie Davis campaign was George Dupuis, the superintendent of schools in Lafayette Parish, Louisiana.

I got to know George when Davis threw me off the campaign bus because I insisted that he talk to reporters. It was in the middle of the night and fifty miles from any city. I was on a narrow two-lane road that ran through pine trees. I see a strip of stars over my head and that was it. But I was glad to be off the damn bus.

I'm standing there with nothing but crickets and mosquitoes for about ten minutes, when I remember I have a cigar in my pocket. I lit up a cigar and started smoking it to keep the mosquitoes off. And then I see some lights coming way back behind over the hill. I stood out in the middle of the road to stop the car, thinking I can hitch a ride.

It turned out to be George in his old Buick. He followed the campaign bus around with a machine gun because he thought people were going to try to do Jimmy in. He had it in the back seat, along with a massive ice box. The box was about four or five feet long, filled with beer and ice.

He asked, "Why you out here on the highway?"

I said, "The governor threw me off the bus."

He said, "Well, we'll follow him and he'll forget about it by tomorrow morning. Get in and have a beer."

So, we drove along and we drank beer.

As Davis' regular antics continued, George and I started traveling together in the old Buick. It was beat up so much because he was drunk so much. But it made the traveling easier for me.

On the last day of the campaign, George and I were in his Buick, driving to the final rally. There was a big field of candidates in that race, more than a dozen. So, there were yard signs everywhere for Edwin Edwards, Bennett Johnson, Gillis Long and the others—big yard signs on a stake.

Now, the Long people were playing with the Davis people. They'd found out where the Davis rally was going to be and lined the roads on both sides with their signs. George, who was two-thirds drunk, took the Buick, put two wheels on the pavement, two wheels on the grass, and ran down those signs. He'd hit them, and they'd fly over the top of the car, one after the other, and he would laugh.

But then we came to a bend in the road. In Louisiana, to make the highway in a lot of places, you got to dig down deep on both sides of the road and pile up the dirt, and it makes pits that fill up with water.

So, the highway turned and we didn't. We go riding off into the water. The water wasn't very deep, when it came up into the car it ran up just to my ankles before it stopped. We slowly settled down into the mud.

We didn't get hurt.

George said, "See if the beer's hurt!"

I look back there and I said, "The beer's fine."

"Okay, see if you can slide it out that back door."

I slid the massive ice box out and we dragged to the pavement.

George said, "Let's stop a car and tell them to call a wrecker."

So, we sat there on the ice box and drank beer.

A wrecker came and pulled the Buick out of the mud.

George said, "We got to sit in the Buick."

The drive of the wrecker said, "You can't do it, it's against the law."

"No, we got to sit in the Buick."

"You can't do that."

Finally, George said, "Look, here's a hundred bucks. We're sitting in the damn Buick."

So, we sat in the Buick for forty miles, drinking beer, while he towed us into a salvage yard.*

---

*For related material and parts of this story, see Strother, *Falling Up*, 80, 84.

Good Old Boy with Bad Habits

Raymond Strother

My partner and I did not do Edwin Edwards' first campaign for governor of Louisiana. He won the primary handedly, then won the runoff narrowly. He forgave that I dropped him during the first campaign and hired me when he ran for a second term. Personally, he and I got along very well—when he ran and didn't run. It was an interesting journey that didn't end well for him.

Edwards was a great campaigner. He started out as a Pentecostal preacher when he was nine years old. He turned Catholic later, but had a great speaking style and a gift for one-liners. He also had a great personal style. He had a guy in Lafayette, Louisiana, the only place he'd buy his suits. The suits were always shiny and they had peculiarities, like cuffs in the sleeves with big brass buttons. He was always different.

One problem was he just loved women beyond belief and constantly chased them. In Louisiana, they called him the "Golden Zipper."

One time during his first re-election race there was a big fundraiser for him in New Orleans where he was going to speak. I went with him. There were about a couple of hundred people in the room and a podium in the front. Just as he started speaking, the most beautiful woman I had ever seen walked in. She was seductively dressed. She walked down the center aisle slowly, turned right in front of the podium, and sat down in the front row. She was obviously one of Edward's girlfriends. Edwin stopped speaking and said, "Hey, hey! She didn't come for me. I think she's here for Strother."

My wife was already a little upset with me for running around the state with Edwards and that comment didn't help.

Edwards also loved gambling and he made no bones about it. He would go to Las Vegas and gamble. The reporters found out about it. They had somebody sneak a camera into a casino and take a picture of him shooting dice. So, in his weekly press conference, a reporter asked, "Governor, there's a rumor that you gamble." He said, "Oh yeah, I'm pretty good at it. I was in Vegas last week, I won ten grand. Next question."

There are many of these kinds of stories about Edwards. They endeared him with the public. It's like Trump, many people did not really care about Edwards' failings. Many people enjoyed a good old boy with bad habits.

But he didn't drink at all. He never had a drink that I knew of.

Besides campaigning, Edwards was great retail politician. He was good at finding allies, making deals, and getting things done. But there was often a whiff of scandal about these things.

Edwards was very popular in his first two terms. Oil prices were high, gas prices were high, production was high, and the state had a lot of money. He increased education spending, university education, and he built lots of roads. So, he did a lot of things and he made a lot of people happy.

Edwards was barred from running for a consecutive third term, but everybody knew he wanted to be governor again. He was sort of a "governor in waiting," while David Treen served as the first Republican governor of the state. Edwards had beaten Treen for his own second term, and when Treen ran for re-election, Edwards beat him again for his third term as governor. They were contrasts—Edwards was colorful and slick, Treen was low key and strait laced. They hated each other.

Edwards' third term did not go well. Oil prices fell and so did state revenues. He got the state legislature to raise taxes and that was very unpopular with the public.

In addition, Edwards and one of his brothers were indicted on federal corruptions charges. Although they both beat the rap, the trial highlighted Edwards' vices, especially his gambling. Then, of all things, he proposed casino gambling and a state lottery in Louisiana to help the state budget.

By the end of his third term, Edwards was very unpopular. So, he drew a large number of credible primary opponents who thought they could beat him for re-election. One was Congressman Buddy Roemer, whom I was representing. This was interesting because Buddy's dad, also called Buddy, had been Edward's campaign manager when he was first elected governor. Edwin and Buddy were friendly rivals.

The whole race was about who would face Edwards in the runoff. There was a debate right before the election where all the candidates were asked if they would endorse Edwards, if as expected, he finished first in the primary. Most tried to sidestep the question, but Roemer said: "No, we've got to slay the dragon. I would endorse anyone but Edwards."

Roemer finished first in the primary ahead of Edwards, Edwards could see the handwriting on the wall. He knew he was not going to beat Roemer, so he withdrew from the runoff election. Roemer automatically became governor.

At that moment, Edwards started working on the legislature, which he still owned, and he put Roemer in a position that he couldn't pass anything unless Edward said he wanted it. Just as before, most people believed Edwards was going to try for another comeback as governor. So, Roemer's agenda mostly went nowhere. He managed to run afoul of the abortion issue by vetoing a strict pro-life bill. He also tried to raise taxes and expand gambling to help with the state budget.

Edwards did try another comeback. The main candidates were Edwards, Roemer, and David Duke, a former Grand Wizard of the Ku Klux Klan. I was then representing Roemer for his re-election bid.

I was then separated from my wife and Roemer asked me to move into the mansion. So, I moved into the governor's mansion.

Louisiana government is high style because you have convicts everywhere, doing everything. You leave your shoes out, they're shined every night. They have a dry-cleaning operation down in the basement. They have twenty-four-hour cooks and bakers. There was always a little ice bucket of milk and two chocolate chip cookies when I went to bed every night. It was terrific.

Living there, I wouldn't campaign twenty-four hours a day. I'd go off and see friends, eat dinner with people, or go to New Orleans. I'd come in every night and the state policeman would wave me through and I'd go to my room. One night I came in and the policeman said, "Mr. Strother, the governor asked that you go to the third floor. They're up there playing cards."

So, I get in the elevator and go up the third floor into the card room. There's Edwards playing poker with Roemer, two or three of Roemer's big contributors, and two or three other local guys I knew. All just playing poker. They're still they're running against each other, head-to-head, and they're playing poker with each other upstairs. It was eye-opening to say the least. I didn't stay long—and it cost me a thousand dollars.

I walked in the mansion one night later on, and I saw Mary Matalin from the Republican National Committee, four of the most prominent Republicans in the state, consultant Harris Diamond from New York, and some other people.

Buddy rushed out of the room and said, "Hey, hey, come into my office." He had a little office downstairs.

He took me in and said, "These guys wanted to talk to me and I had to be gracious. I had to say they could come."

I said, "Buddy, are you turning Republican?"

"No, no, no man, don't worry about that. But when the president of the United States calls, are you going to tell the president of the United States, 'No, I won't see any of your friends?'" The first President Bush was then in the White House.

He said, "Go on to bed and don't worry about it."

Actually, Roemer had big aspirations. He wanted to run for president himself, which he did eventually. He thought the Democrats were going down the tubes.

So, the next morning, I woke up, got on my plane, and flew to Texas, where I represented Governor Mark White. I was in Austin when I picked up the *Austin American*. There on page two I read "Governor of Louisiana changes parties." This was several months before the primary. The timing dismayed both Democrats and Republicans. I had this terrible "What do I do?" moment.

Two, three days later, I packed myself up and went back to Washington D.C.

Then Buddy called and asked, "Where are you?"

I said, "Buddy, you're a Republican, I'm a Democrat."

"Oh man, think about who you're running against. The corruption of Edwin Edwards and racism of David Duke. Do you think I'm the best or the worst of that group?"

"Oh, you're a hundred times better than either of them."

"So, you'll ditch me? I'm your friend and you'll ditch me because of what, I put an R behind my name instead of a D? I'm still pro-choice." He went on through the whole thing.

"I'll think about it," I said.

So, anyway, I ended up going back to him and doing the campaign.

I did all kinds of research about David Duke. I had this Republican firm doing focus groups. I was sitting there in enemy territory, really, and they would describe David Duke to the focus groups. The focus groups said, "Oh man, a racist, I couldn't support him at all, he's awful. No, no, no David Duke." We did four focus groups and we couldn't find a single person who'd support David Duke.

The focus group guy came out of the room and said, "I don't think you boys have any trouble with David Duke."

I said, "You didn't ask the question right. In this next group, do it this way. Don't ask who they're supporting, ask who their neighbor is supporting, people who live on both sides. Ask that." He went back in and the group said, "My neighbors, they're supporting Duke. Everybody I know is supporting Duke."

The focus group guy came back in and said, "We got big trouble."

But in these focus groups, I found out how to beat Duke. I found out if Buddy would take Duke head on and say, "Duke's going to be bad for the economy," Roemer could win.

I told Buddy, "Let me make some commercials with waiters and hotel bellhops in New Orleans saying I'll lose my job because we won't have any tourists. Let me go up to north Louisiana and make an economic appeal out of it."

He said, "No, I don't want to make any Republicans mad at me this moment. I'm going to need every one of them I can get because I lost all the Black vote."

I said, "Well, you're going to lose."

He said, "Well, sometimes you win, sometimes you lose."

Sure enough, Buddy lost. He finished third behind Duke, who was second, and Edwards, who was first. It was Edwards and Duke in the runoff. I packed up the next day and flew back to Washington D.C.

That night Edwards called me.

He says, "Raymond, I understand you have some information about how to beat David Duke? Talk to me about it." I talked to him about it for a while.

He said, "Very interesting."

I said, "I have some polls too."

He said, "Very interesting. Talk to Bill Morgan."

Well, Bill Morgan had worked for me and had left me to go work for Edwards' campaign. So, Bill called me and said, "I'm going to the football game, and I know you've got the governor's box." I still had the governor's box for another week or two in the Superdome.

He said, "Our box is next door, why don't we meet there so nobody knows what we're doing."

So, I went to New Orleans, there's Morgan, and we drove back to Baton Rouge together and outlined everything that I'd learned about the David Duke operation, and how to beat him.

I laid it out, he said, "Good."

Then, that night or the night after that, I got a call from the publisher of the *Times-Picayune* newspaper, Ashton Phelps. He said, "Raymond, the governor tells me you know how to beat this David Duke. We can't have him win. It would wreck our state."

I said, "Yeah, it would."

So, I went through the whole thing with Ashton Phelps, and he said, "Let me tell you what I'm going to do. I'm going to turn the entire resources of our newspaper to beating David Duke. If you see any way that I can do a better job, you call me, and I'll do it."

I never called; I never did anything.

Then Edwards got mad at me because I had not done his campaign, that I'd stayed with Roemer. He got angry with me because I didn't come with him into the runoff.

I was tired, beat up, and my wife was trying to come home. I just didn't want to do his campaign. I just didn't want to do it.

Edwards beat David Duke going away in the runoff. Everybody was afraid they were going to lose their jobs if Duke won. Everybody who was anybody backed Edwards—even David Treen and Buddy Roemer.

My marriage improved, but Edwards' fortunes did not. His fourth term was wracked by scandal. He went to jail right after he left office for the last time.[*]

---

[*]For material related to this story, see Strother, *Falling Up,* 231–233, 248–262.

Protecting the Institution
Raymond Strother

I first got to Washington D.C. in 1980 at the behest of Senator Russell Long, the son of Governor Huey Long, nicknamed "The Kingfish," who was legendary in Louisiana politics in the 1920s and 1930s.

Senator Long was the chairman of the Finance Committee. He knew how to use the power of the position. President John F. Kennedy called him the most powerful man in America because when he was asked one time if he was going to do something, he said, "I don't know, I'll have to ask Senator Long if I may." Before I produced media for his campaign in 1980, Senator Long had never been seriously challenged.

Senator Long loved the United States Senate. He thought the institution itself was incredibly important. He was worried about one of his brethren, Senator John Stennis from Mississippi. Senator Stennis had served forty-one years and was senior member in the Senate. Like Long, Senator Stennis had never been challenged. The most money he had spent in a campaign was barely more than his filing fee. He was loved in Mississippi.

Senator Long came to me one day and he said, "Raymond, I want you to go over and talk to Senator Stennis; he's gonna need your help. He's got this fella named Haley Barbour running against him. We don't know him, he's a kid."

But, he said, "It's gonna be a real campaign and Senator Stennis doesn't know how to do it."

So, I went over to see John Stennis and he said, "What is it you do, sir?" He was very formal. I tried to explain political consulting in two minutes and he stopped me and he says, "I understand, you're a photographer."

I said, "Well yeah, I'm a photographer." I just let it go at that.

He said, "I see," he said, "Well tell me this, do you take the pictures that are all run together or take pictures you look at one at a time?"

I said, "All run together."

He said, "Don't have much luck with that."

Then he said, "I send those things down to Mississippi. I don't think anybody runs them. I make 'em down below the Senate chambers in the studio. But I don't think anybody runs them."

I said, "Senator, we pay the stations to run them."

He was astonished, "You pay them? I guess that would change things."

I said, "Yes, that would change things a lot."

He said, "Well, well, well, very good."

We had idle conversation about Senator Long and I soon left. He had Senate business.

About a day or two later, I got a call from a secretary, "Mr. Strother, this is so-and-so, Senator Stennis's office wants to know if you can come over and see him tomorrow at about two o'clock."

I confirmed I would be there at two and called Senator Long and told him about the meeting. He was enthused. He and Senator Lloyd Bentsen had had a talk with Stennis about how serious it was that I be hired.

About ten minutes later, the phone rang. "Mr. Strother, this is Senator John Stennis of Mississippi, you may remember me, I met you with Senator Long."

I said, "I do remember you, Senator."

"I was wondering if we might not get together tomorrow, about two o'clock."

I said, "Yes sir, two o'clock, tomorrow."

He said, "Fine, fine, fine, fine."

Half an hour later the phone rang again.

"Mr. Strother, this is Senator John Stennis of Mississippi, you might remember me; I met you with Senator Long."

Hesitantly, I said, "Yes sir."

"I was wondering if we might not get together tomorrow about two o'clock."

I said, "Yes," completely perplexed.

So, the next day I walked across the capitol campus from my office to the Senate office building. When I walked in his secretary, who's just slightly younger than he, runs up and says, "Are you Mr. Strother?"

I said, "Yes."

And she said, "Oh dear, oh dear, he forgot and went home to take a nap."

I said, "Well, that's ok."

So, I went back to my office. A couple of days later got a call from Senators Long and Bentsen. They said, "Raymond, how's Senator Stennis's campaign going?"

I said, "I don't have any idea. I haven't heard from him."

Senator Bentsen sounded a little aggravated. "You haven't heard from him, you're not hired?"

"No," I said.

Senator Bentsen asked, "What does it take to hire you?"

"Just like our agreement, Senator, just a handshake."

"Huh, this is strange," he said, "OK," and then hung up.

A few minutes later, I got a call, "Mr. Strother, this is Senator John Stennis, from Mississippi. I'm wondering if you couldn't come over to my office to see me right now."

I walked across campus and he was there this time. He leaned over his desk, extended his hand and said, "A firm handshake, sir." And we shook hands. Two firm handshakes.

He said, "OK, how's my campaign going?"

I said, "Senator, your campaign isn't going."

"What do you mean it isn't going?"

"Well, you haven't hired me."

"Oh," he said, "I thought Senator Long hired you. Well, what do I need to do?"

"Well, a handshake would do it."

He said, "Then a firm handshake, sir," and we shook hands again.

And he said, "What else I need to do?"

I said, "Well, you need to pay me."

He said, "Pay you?"

I said, "Yes, sir."

He said, "How much do you want?"

"My base fee is $50,000."

He was astonished. "Sir, I don't have that kind of money. What other money will I need?"

I said, "Well, you'll need about a million dollars for television."

He sat back in his chair, shaking his head. "A million dollars? Sir, a million dollars? If I sold my house, my cars, and took my savings account, I couldn't come up with a million dollars. I don't think I'm gonna be able to run. Oh dear. But it's been good to meet you."

When I got back to my office and Senator Bentsen called me.

He said, "Raymond, please never discuss money with Senator Stennis again. Come to Senator Long or me with your bills. We'll take care of all of that."

Peter Hart was the pollster and did some focus groups. We found that even people who loved Stennis were reluctant to support him when they found that he was eighty-seven years old. He went from seventy percent approval to thirty percent approval in our polls or something like that. They didn't want an old, old man representing Mississippi. But he had never been on television down there and they hadn't seen him forever. We could elect his reputation and record of service, but not the man.

Then I had a scare.

Senator Stennis informed me he was going to the traditional Neshoba County Fair. It was a huge tradition in Mississippi, lasting two or three days. People give political speeches all day. And hundreds and thousands of people line up to listen. I do not know why.

I called Peter Hart in panic. Peter and I met Senator Stennis in his office that afternoon to plead with him to avoid the big press event.

Peter said, "You need to stay up here."

Stennis was offended. He said, "No, that young man, Mr. Barbour, thinks I'm a coward. I'm gonna go down and show Mr. Barbour I'm not a coward. Well, I'm going to the county fair."

"Please don't go there. There will be cameras all over the place. Republicans are going be looking for you. There could be something embarrassing. Don't go."

Peter was gentle in his argument. "Senator, every day you look in the mirror and see the same man. Change comes slowly. However, people in Mississippi have not seen you for thirty years. They will see a huge change."

So, finally, Peter and I talked him out of it.

He looked down at his hands and sadly said, "OK, I won't go."

I was asleep the next night when I got a call from Stennis' press secretary, Rex Buffington.

"I got bad news."

I said, "What's that, Rex?"

He says, "Senator Stennis went to the Neshoba Fair."

I said, "Ohh."

He said, "No, man, it's much worse. When he got there, there was a banner across the entranceway saying 'Happy 87th Birthday, Senator Stennis!'"

I said, "Oh, God."

Rex said, "No, it gets worse, Raymond. Then they had a beautiful little girl bring out a cake with a forest fire on top of it: eighty-seven lit candles."

"Did he accept it?"

"Yes, he was honored and pleased to get the cake with eighty-seven candles."

"Oh man, can it get worse?"

"It can."

"What happened?"

"Well, when he was going up to get up on the podium, he had to go up about six steps, and he fell, and was caught by his opponent, Haley Barbour."

"Did they film it?"

"Oh yeah. Every step of the way, he was filmed with the birthday cake, and they filmed him falling; his knees gave out."

"You don't have any more bad news, do you?"

"Yep."

"What?" I had almost squeezed the phone receiver in half.

"After he got to his chair on the stage and the introduction began, he went to sleep. He slept there for the entire thing."

I said to myself, "Now what do you do now, Mr. Nimble?"

I threw deep. I called the bureau chief on the *New York Times*, who was a friend of mine, and indignantly said, "Did you hear what they did to that poor old man in Mississippi? Those Republicans trying get a film opportunity, pushing him down on the steps. A bunch of damn ruffians!" And I went on and on and on, as though I'd been there.

The next day, a tiny story came out in the *New York Times*, about two paragraphs, about him stumbling on the steps that didn't say ruffians pushed him, but a campaign official said someone pushed him on the stairs. I then copied the story, had it printed and dropped thousands of them out of my airplane all over Mississippi. It was checkmate. They could not use their film.

Senators from both parties loved Stennis. He was their conscience; he was their father. Later, when he retired, I filmed a documentary for a tribute party. By this time, he had lost a leg to diabetes and was in dementia. I did a series of interviews with him and I said, "Senator Stennis, what's the best thing that's happened since you've been in the Senate?"

"The best thing is that Black people and women are involved."

When the film was shown to the elite in Washington D.C., Ronald Reagan was president. And Reagan was there, sitting next to Senator Stennis. The senator kept nodding off at the head table. When Senator Stennis' head would nod, President Reagan would elbow him, wake him up, and whisper into his ear.

I suddenly liked Reagan.

The room was filled with admirals, generals, and lords of industry. Reagan kept the old Senator's attention and would occasionally point to an admiral or general. In his remarks, when Stennis started to repeat himself for the third time, Reagan stood up by him and started applauding. The senator thought he had finished speaking and sat down.

Of course, I never voted for Reagan, and I disagreed with him on almost everything. But his kindness to Senator Stennis that night changed my mind about him. His obvious affection for Stennis was one of the more decent political acts I've ever seen done in my life. Those guys respected each other. I don't see that kind of respect today.*

---

* For related material and parts of this story, see Strother, *Falling Up,* 130–140.

Old Friends Conduct Politics
Raymond Strother

My friendship and successful campaign for Senator Russell Long proved to be the defining event of my professional life. He introduced me to Lloyd Bentsen, Dennis DeConcini, Paul Simon, and a lot of other people. His stamp of approval was pure gold. My current lifestyle is directly attributable to Russell Long, who was my mentor and political father. And, I might modestly add, my friend.

He lived in the Watergate Complex in Washington D.C. and would occasionally call me to join him downstairs at Restaurant John Louis when his wife, Carolyn, was out of town. One afternoon he called, "My secretary tells me your wife's out of town and my wife's out of town, why don't we have dinner?" He called again in an hour later. "Raymond, would it be ok with you if I invited Bob Dole? His wife's out of town." I immediately said I would be honored to join these two masters of the Senate.

Well, Russell Long was Democratic Chairman of finance and Bob Dole was the Republican minority leader on the committee. It was a great dinner. They laughed, told funny political and personal stories while I listened. I kept my mouth shut. There was nothing I could add to these two guys. It was a rather long dinner. Dole had a couple of drinks; Long and I stuck with water. Long, once a prodigious drinker had stopped drinking years before, and I had a rule to never drink with a client.

When the check was paid and Long pushed back his chair, Dole grabbed him with whichever was his good arm—he had been seriously wounded in WWII in the other arm.

"Russell, Russell, before we go, we've had that tax bill in committee now for months. Let's get that out of the way."

Dole said, "I'll give you A, B, and F, if you give me D, C, and E."

Long said, "Uhhhh, OK."

They shook hands. The next day, the bill came out of committee. I had just witnessed a major political dilemma solved by good friends from opposing parties.

That's how people worked then. That doesn't happen today.

Gary Hart Makes a Call
Raymond Strother

The top rung of any consultant's success ladder is a presidential campaign. . .any presidential campaign.

Though I had big ambitions when I moved to Washington D.C. from Louisiana in 1980, I did not have the audacity to even consider a lofty presidential campaign— until Gary Hart walked over to my office on New Jersey Avenue. He had called and said he would walk over and wanted to see my work. So, I arranged my various campaign tapes and put on a fresh pot of coffee.

Later I found that Senator Lloyd Bentsen of Texas had asked him to talk to me before he hired a consultant for the 1984 presidential campaign. But, until he called, I had no intention on trying to sell my services to his campaign.

Televisions weren't as large as they are now, so the television and recorder were behind my desk on a bookshelf. I arranged all the tapes I wanted to show him in order on the bookshelf. But the hinges came off of my planned presentation when Hart asked, "Why would you want to be involved in my campaign?"

I was startled and his quick question unlocked emotions I normally hid. "Because of my brother. He died in Vietnam and you were one of the only politicians to have the guts to say it was the wrong war and not worth the loss of my brother."

He sincerely said, "Oh, I'm sorry."

That's when I lost it. "Yeah and I'm still pissed off."

I went into a rant that I shouldn't have done about Vietnam about the idiots that put us in that war. I must have ranted for ten minutes. After the emotional dust had settled, Hart sat and talked to me for two hours about foreign policy, about Vietnam, and then abruptly, he said, "Well, I gotta go."

I said, "You haven't looked at my work?"

He said, "That's ok." He left.

Well, I never thought I'd get a presidential campaign, anyway, so it didn't disappoint me. I turned around and went back to work on my novel, *Cottonwood*.

Within twenty-four hours Billy Shore called me, "Raymond, Senator Hart said to get together and work out the contract for his presidential race."

I was astonished. "Are you kidding me?"

"No, you're hired. If you take the campaign there won't be a fee, but he will allow full commissions."

So, Hart and I started our long journey, and with Hart, it was a *long* journey. He was a very difficult man to deal with because he's an intellectual.

The next time we met, he asked, "How are you going to betray me?"

I said, "I'm not going to betray you. I'm going to let you be who you are. And I'm going to film you speaking off the cuff and I will take the parts of it that work and put them on the air. I don't think I can really write for you."

He answered, "Perfect. You're not going to script me?"

I said, "I'm not going to script you at all."

I remember he smiled, "That's the way I want media to be done."

So, we started off on our journey like that. And it worked very well. The campaign changed my business and my life.

Walter Mondale, of course, narrowly defeated Hart in the 1984 Democratic primaries. Except for some bonehead moves on the campaign's part and his part, Hart almost won the nomination. He wasn't really damaged by the 1984 campaign because he didn't expect to win. He got into it knowing that it was the setup to the next presidential race, because if he won the nomination, he was gonna have to run against Ronald Reagan for second term. We all knew he couldn't beat Reagan. He never admitted that to me, incidentally, but it was obvious. He wasn't disappointed in losing the primary to Mondale at all—in fact, he liked Mondale.

We continued our journey as he got ready to run for the 1988 Democratic nomination.*

---

* For related material and parts of this story, see Strother, *Falling Up*, 169–174, 202–203.

Gary Hart Makes a Decision
Raymond Strother

About two or three years after the 1984 campaign, I said to Senator Hart, "You know, I would really like to put you together with my client, Bill Clinton." I represented Clinton in Arkansas.

He said, "I think I know him; he worked for the McGovern campaign."

"Yeah, he did."

"Yeah, I think I know him. I have never really spent any time with him."

"Let's go down and talk to him. "I can't imagine a better ticket: a Southerner and you. He could be your vice president."

"Well, I'd be happy to talk to him."

So, Hart arranged a private plane to fly us to Arkansas. A state trooper came out, picked us up, took us to the governor's mansion in Little Rock for lunch. We stayed about an hour and a half. Then we got back got back in a squad car and drove back to the airport.

Gary was just looking out the car window.

Now, what you have to remember about Hart is that is that he's not a man of words—he doesn't speak a lot. There are these long silences. Sometimes I'd ride with him on airplanes, sitting in the next seat for three hours, and we'd never speak—not one word. A quiet man.

So, he was just looking out the window on the way to the airport. After about thirty minutes, I couldn't bear it any longer.

I said, "Gary, what did you think?"

"About what?"

"About Governor Clinton."

"He doesn't stand for anything."

End of conversation.

End of Bill Clinton's association with Gary Hart.*

---

*For an earlier version of this story, see Strother, *Falling Up,* 214.

Gary Hart is Set Up
Raymond Strother

The whole Hart carnival came to an end on a boat named the *Monkey Business*. Here's how it happened.

One day as we were gearing up for the 1988 campaign, Gary Hart says to me, "You know, I need to expand my fundraising team and I need somebody that can help me raise money in the South. Do you know anybody?"

I said, "Yeah. My guy Billy Broadhurst is a good fundraiser and he can raise a lot of money out of the oil patch in Louisiana."

I knew Broadhurst from Louisiana politics. He had moved to Washington D.C. to open a lobbying firm because he had a good association with Senator John Breaux, and before that, Senator Russell Long. So, he had the basis for a lobbying business.

Billy was a "hail fellow well met." He had a beautiful home a couple of blocks behind the Supreme Court building. And he would ask me over in the afternoon for drinks.

"Why don't I put a dinner together at his house?" I said to Hart. "He has a Cajun chef at his house and he'll cook a fabulous dinner." Hart wasn't a big food guy, really, so that didn't matter much, but he said, "That's good."

So, I put together the dinner. Hart and Broadhurst got along very well—famously, in fact. Eventually Broadhurst got to be Hart's traveling companion and they traveled together all the time.

At that time, I represented Annette Strauss, who was running for mayor of Dallas, Texas. She was the sister-in-law of Bob Strauss, the former chair of the Democratic National Committee.

Strauss had called me and said, "Raymond, I want you to do this race."

I said, "I don't do mayors."

At the time I didn't—I only did popes and kings and presidents. Besides the mayor of Dallas was a nothing position at the time, with no power. It's a ceremonial position. I don't even know why anyone would want to be mayor of Dallas.

He said, "No, you wanna do it."

I said "Ok" because no one said no to Bob Strauss in the Democratic establishment.

So, fast-forward to Billy Broadhurst and Gary Hart.

Billy calls me and said, "Hey Raymond," he said, "You and Gary are working on that speech he's gonna give at Yale?"

I said, "Yeah."

He said, "Well, that's great. I've rented a boat down in Florida, and I'm gonna take Gary out to the Bimini or someplace out there in the Bahamas. He wants to work on that speech; you come along and the two of you can work on the speech."

Then Billy said, "The reason I want you there is I have a bill-fishing boat and I want to go fishing. And you're a fisherman. You and I will go bill-fishing for swordfish."

Hart didn't fish or hunt or anything like that.

I said, "Yeah, great."

So, I got on the phone, called Delta airlines, and booked me a ticket to Lauderdale.

About a day or so later, Annette Strauss called me. She's weeping and she said, "Raymond, they've attacked me viciously here in Dallas."

I said, "On television?"

"Yes, on television."

My media buyer hasn't alerted me about any negative television buy or any television.

I said, "What station?"

She said, "Oh, channel 63."

"Oh, don't worry about that," I said, "It's a minor station."

She said, "You've got to come down here."

I said, "No, Annette, I can't; I have other plans; I can't come down."

"Please come."

"No, no, I won't, I can't. I hope you understand, but, you know, you're fine; don't worry about it."

We had found out that only twenty percent of the people in Dallas voted for the mayor. So, we lined up the gays, the Hispanics, the unions—and just with those, we could get twenty percent of the vote in Dallas. There was nothing to worry about.

The telephone rings about an hour later, "Raymond, Bob Strauss."

I said, "Yes, sir?"

He said, "Get your ass to Dallas."

"Bob," I said, "I've got other things I need to do."

"Raymond, get your ass to Dallas."

I said, "Yes, sir."

So, I call Broadhurst and I said, "I can't go with you and Gary on that boat ride. I've got to go to Dallas."

Billy and Gary get to Lauderdale and the boat that had been booked by Broadhurst. The captain tells them, "I'm sorry, this boat can't sail; it's out of commission. But I've got another boat for you across the way."

So, they go to another marina a few miles away to a boat called the *Monkey Business*. And they go on board and they're having cocktails that night; they're gonna leave the next morning for Bimini at first light.

The there's a rap on the side of the boat. There are two women, one is named Lynn Armandt and one is named Donna Rice, and two men. Lynn Armandt, who is the spokesperson, said, "Oh, a friend of ours owns this boat. Would you mind if we showed our boyfriends around a little bit? Let them see it?"

Billy said, "Ah, come on board." So, they came on board and joined Billy and Gary for a couple drinks. To make a long story short, the visitors ended up going to Bimini with them the next day. During the trip, Lynn Armandt shoves Donna Rice into Gary's lap, laughing, "Hahaha," and takes a picture.

That picture would be seen over the world very shortly, courtesy of the *National Inquirer*.

It was a setup. I knew it was a setup. ABC News knew it was a setup, and they tried to prove it, and finally, after many months of reporting, their attorneys pulled them off the story.

The Republican operative Lee Atwater had arranged for the first boat to be disabled and had rented the second boat. The deal was Lynn Armandt's boyfriend was going to get out of prison for dealing cocaine. Before Lee Atwater died, he confessed to me that he set that thing up.[*]

When ABC dug into the story, they found that Lynn Armandt and Donna Rice had also been in Denver two weeks earlier at a reception of Hart. And Hart was standing right next to his wife and they shook hands with him and never had any other contact. Hart didn't even recognize who they were when they came on the boat. So that scene in Fort Lauderdale was the second time they had taken a shot at Hart.

Annette Strauss was comfortably elected mayor of Dallas and Gary Hart's presidential campaign began an agonizing collapse.[**]

---

[*] James Fallows, "Was Gary Hart Set Up?" *The Atlantic*, November 2018.
[**] For material related to this story, see Strother, *Falling Up*, 235–237.

Mark of a Losing Campaign
Raymond Strother

In 1988, I was representing Senator Lloyd Bentsen for re-election to the United States Senate, as I had done before. And then he was nominated for vice president. All of a sudden, I'm doing a senate campaign and a vice-presidential campaign. Texas is unusual in this regard—Senator Lyndon Johnson did the same thing when he ran for re-election and vice president in 1960.

But I'm not doing much of a vice-presidential campaign because there isn't much to do. The people from Boston controlled everything and held everything very tightly—much as the Hillary Clinton people did in the 2016 campaign.

Senator Bentsen came to me one day and said, "Raymond, the Republicans are going to blast us on gun control. You know where I stand, I own shotguns." He was a skeet-shooting champion.

"The only person in this race who's ever voted for gun control is George Bush. I want you to make a television spot saying that." Of course, Bush was the Republican presidential nominee in 1988. He had lost the 1970 U.S. Senate race in Texas to Bentsen.

So, I made a spot and took it to him. He said, "That's good, Raymond, it's just exactly what I wanted. Send it to Boston and get them to approve it. They want to approve everything we do. Send it to Boston and get it approved, and we'll put it on the air in Texas next week."

The senator called me the next week, "Raymond, when's the spot going up?"

"Senator, I haven't heard from Boston."

"That's strange, they told me they'd get to you, but okay."

He called me a week later, "Raymond, tell me about the spot."

"I still haven't heard from them."

"Well, that's strange, they told me again that they'd call you. Where are you? I'll call you back in thirty minutes wherever you're going to be."

I gave him my number—we didn't have cell phones in 1988.

He called me back and said, "Okay, there's a guy at campaign headquarters. He's going to be expecting your call at 12:05 eastern time."

So, I'm riding around looking for locations in Austin with one of the senator's aides. I kept looking at the clock. Then I said, "Okay, find a payphone." She found a park in Austin with a payphone on a pole and pulled over. I called Boston at exactly 12:05 p.m.

Somebody answered the phone, I told them who I was and who I needed to speak with.

The person said, "Well, he's not available."

"No, No, he's expecting me, I'm supposed to call at exactly this time. He's expecting my call."

"Well, let me go see."

The person came back on the line and said, "No, he's busy, he can't talk to you."

"Did you talk to him?"

"No, I talked to someone who works for him, and he can't talk to you, he's busy."

"Senator Bentsen said he was going to talk to me at this time. I want to speak to him. Now. Because I'm going to get in trouble with Senator Bentsen."

So, the guy comes on the phone and identifies himself. I don't know who he was—and to this day I don't know who he was.

"Hello, who are you?"

So, I went through who I was, name, rank, serial number.

He said, "Look sport, I never heard of you, don't call this number again. Go f**k yourself." And hung up.

I was so angry that I don't know what to do. I stumbled back to the car where the aide is waiting. I told her what happened and she shook her head. She had a bulky car phone with two or three channels. She was one of the few people who had the telephone number for the presidential campaign plane, where Bentsen was traveling with Governor Dukakis.

So, she calls Bentsen and said "Senator, you need to hear this directly from Raymond," and hands the car phone to me. I went through the whole conversation.

In pure Bentsen fashion he said, "Uh-huh, well, well."

Then he said, "Raymond, don't worry about it, it's all over anyway."

It was a three or so weeks before the election. He knew the mark of a losing campaign.*

---

*For an earlier version of this story, see Strother, *Falling Up,* 9.

Where Credit is Due

Raymond Strother

Senator Bentsen was prepping for a debate with Dan Quayle, the Republican vice-presidential nominee in 1988. We were going to do our debate coaching in a small auditorium at the Four Seasons Hotel in Austin, Texas. We were feeling some pressure because Quayle was a made-for-television candidate.

Bentsen had very specific instructions.

"Ok," he said, "Here's who I want to come with me: Michael Sheen (a Democratic speech coach who was working for us), Jack Martin (the press secretary), and Raymond."

We did exactly what Bentsen said. But when we got to the auditorium, it was jammed with the Dukakis people.

It did not go well.

The moderator would ask Bentsen a question. When he started answering it, somebody in the back would say, "Wait, wait, wait, Senator, you are off message. That—no, no, no, that won't do. Here's what you have to say."

Then they'd go on for five minutes about what to say.

When Bentsen said, "Okay, next question," the process was repeated.

"No, no, no, Senator," somebody else over there would say, "the tone is wrong. Here's what you've got to say."

This went on about ten minutes.

I could see the anger rising in Bentsen. He believed, like most Texans, that you don't show your whole card, you don't show your anger. But I knew him. I knew what was going on in his head.

He was a very dignified, elegant, strong man. These critics were pipsqueaks and he knew they were pipsqueaks. They didn't have any real power or responsibility.

Bentsen closed his briefing book.

Then the debate coach Michael Sheen spoke up, "Senator, Senator, I've got an idea. You know, Quayle is always comparing himself to John Kennedy. I wrote this little line out: 'Senator, I knew John Kennedy. John Kennedy was a friend of mine. You're no John Kennedy.' You could use it someplace in the debate."

Bentsen said, "That's it, I'm gone."

And he walked out of the auditorium.

I turned to Jack Martin and said, "What?"

"Bentsen didn't like that," he said, "He didn't like the line; he didn't like the suggestion. He didn't like the way he was treated here." And so forth.

So, we're in the greenroom in Omaha, Nebraska watching the vice-presidential debate. All of the sudden, Bentsen uses Michael Sheen's line.

I sat forward in surprise.

Bentsen had no respect for Quayle whatsoever. He didn't consider him smart enough to be up there on a national ticket. He had disdain for Quayle, and finally Quayle just pushed him too far.

Bentsen took Michael Sheen's line and used it.

Everybody associated with the campaign has taken credit for that line, except me and Michael Sheen—the person who gave it to him.

Crazy
Raymond Strother

An old friend of mine, who was a state labor leader, called and said, "I want you to go talk to this fellow who wants to run for office." I told him I'd be happy to make the meeting. He'd directed several campaigns to me in my early days and I owed him. So, I flew from Washington D.C. to see his candidate and he was pretty impressive. He knew why he was running and could articulate it. I took his campaign.

After three or four visits, the people closest to him called me in and said, "You've got to help us."

"What's wrong?"

"We've got a bad girlfriend problem."

"Well, I've run into that."

"No, no, you don't understand, this girl is crazy. She's completely crazy. She's threatening to call the press and expose their relationship, which is about five years old."

"What can I do?"

"You've got to go down and talk to her."

So, I got in my plane, went down to the city, and made arrangements to have lunch with her.

She was an attractive woman, not a girl, maybe thirty years old. Everything about her was classy. She sat down and started a conversation. She was articulate and knew a lot about politics.

After an hour, I was thinking, "Wow, these people are so wrong about this woman. I don't know how we're going to handle it, but this woman isn't a threat to the campaign."

This opinion unraveled with dessert.

She said, "Now, I've got to share something with you."

"What's that?"

"Your candidate is crazy."

"What do you mean?"

"Well, he rode in a parade with his family," she declared and leaned back.

"Yeah?" Seemed okay to me.

She said again with emphasis, "With his family!"

I guess I nodded. I didn't know what to say.

She went on, "Everybody knows about us, why did he show up with his family?"

I finally understood and said with the same drama she used, "Oh my gosh, I can't imagine doing something like that."

I was getting the drift.

She *was* crazy.

"I'm going to tell you something worse than that," she continued, "He got a new car, a Buick, and he wouldn't have the windows tinted so people couldn't see as we drove around town. Do you think that's crazy?"

"Oh yeah. now I understand."

"I'll tell you, he's even crazier than that. I'm a good-looking woman."

"You are."

Getting a little loud, she continued, "We go to a restaurant, you know where we sit? He always has a private room, a private room."

"He is truly crazy."

"Oh insane, just completely insane."

Then she said, "I'm going to stop it, he's just too crazy to serve in office. I'm going to make sure he isn't going to get there."

I held up my hand like I was trying to flag down a speeding train.

"Wait, wait, wait, why don't we work together?" I said, "You don't have to do this. You'll get over this tomorrow and you'll feel better."

She said, "Yeah, sometimes I get angry and sometimes I'm not angry."

That comment made me dizzy.

After I had calmed her down a bit, we were beginning to attract attention. I said, "I'll tell you what, I have a private number in my library in Washington D.C. Nobody has the number, even my wife. I'm going to write it out for you on my card. Any time you feel like you've been wronged, let's talk it over."

For the rest of the campaign, at four a.m. or three a.m., my library phone would ring. My wife would turn over and say, "The crazy woman is on the line." And I'd run into the library from the bedroom next door. She was usually crying, telling me something awful that my candidate had done. I would spend hours talking to her.

But she never went public.

When the candidate was elected, I went to him and I said, "You know, in this state there's a law that the coroner can commit your girlfriend—deem her insane and put her away."

"Oh, no man. Don't do that. I'll break it off with her. I promise I'll break it off with her, don't do that." He knew the coroner and I were very good friends. He said, "Don't call." He was weeping.

I said, "Okay, I'll give you two weeks to break it off." But he didn't break it off immediately, it festered on and off for months. Meanwhile, the candidate was getting ready to run for a statewide office.

As the next campaign got underway, I would occasionally visit the candidate. I was talking to him and a young female intern walked down the hall to his office.

He said, "You see that?"

I said, "Yeah, I see that."

"She's something, man. You know, I'm getting close to that. I've taken her to dinner twice and for drinks a couple of times. I'm getting close to that."

"Don't, don't, don't, man! We're trying to solve the old problem."

"No, I'm never going to see the crazy woman again. Don't worry about it. But this girl is different."

"Oh, man." He *was* crazy.

Finally, it solved itself with another problem.

After a few months, when the candidate began to organize his statewide campaign, we did some negative research, and found he had some really serious financial problems. It looked like jail time to me. I resigned.

A few days later he calls all his money people in the room to talk to me. They used every argument to say, "You're not going to resign."

"Yes, I've resigned. I'll go to the jailhouse door with any client but I won't go inside. I'm through."

I soon had another client who beat him in a primary. The crazy woman never showed up. But he was crazy enough to trade one problem for another.

Dwarf Luck
Raymond Strother

In the mid-1990s, I was brought into the Dominican Republic by Bill Hamilton, the pollster, who was working a lot there for a guy named Jacinto Peynado. Jacinto was running for vice president with the acquiescence of President Joaquin Balaguer, the old, blind dictator, who didn't call himself a dictator. He was almost mystical to a lot of the people on the island.

I was going back and forth to the Dominican Republic organizing media for Jacinto with a pollster Hamilton assigned to be my assistant. We were caged in a resort called "The Jaguar." It was on the ocean with a beautiful swimming pool complex plus a restaurant and a rather large casino downstairs.

We immediately began to say to each other that the Dominican Republic was not like doing a campaign in Kansas—it was completely different. For example, when we went to see Jacinto, we had to have armed guards, since the gringos were always a little in danger if they were doing campaigns.

Our meetings were usually held at Jacinto's house. He lived in a compound in the middle of the city—and not necessarily a good part of town—that was almost a full block, surrounded by a large wall with barbed wire on top. He had a guard with a shotgun on each corner.

Jacinto was a big political figure so a lot of the people gathered around the main gate when the car would go in. They would smuggle a piece of paper in your hand asking, "I need a new refrigerator" or "I need a new stove." You knew they were looking for political favors.

Jacinto was a rich man. He owned orange groves, old cigar factories, Toyota dealerships, and a lot of other things. He had a jet helicopter, a Learjet, and also had a beautiful condo in Miami. He had been educated at the Wharton School. He was a very bright and jovial man of about 330 pounds. I liked him very much.

So, two guys with automatic weapons in a Toyota bus picked us up every morning and carried us to Jacinto's compound. I liked Santo Domingo, I found it interesting. We'd go the same route every day, and every day we went by the presidential mansion where Balaguer lived with his sister. When we went by there were always two dwarves sweeping sidewalks out front, a man and a woman, who looked fairly old.

One day, I couldn't stand it any longer.

I said, "Jacinto, why are there two dwarves sweeping in front of the president's house?"

He said, "They're on retainers for Balaguer. They worked for him for many decades. You know in the Dominican Republic people consider dwarves mystical and magical and bring good luck. All rich people have a dwarf working for them. just in case it's true."

I asked, "You're a rich man. Do you have a dwarf?"

He said, "Oh, yeah. I have one working for me at the Toyota dealership."

I said, "Do they bring luck?"

He said, "I think so, I think they help you with luck. A lot of people like to gamble with a dwarf."

I said, "Well, what if I shot dice?"

He said, "Oh, I think they'd help you with dice."

I said, "That's interesting. One day lend me your dwarf, if you would, to gamble in the casino downstairs."

"Yeah," he said.

I was sure that was the end of it. Then we had a long political discussion. We were planning a campaign.

We finished our meeting and went back the hotel to take a nap. At an appointed hour, we met at the elevator to go to a Spanish restaurant we liked for dinner.

When the elevator door opened on the first floor, there was a huge man holding a dwarf under his arm.

He said, "Mr. Raymond, I brought you your dwarf."

I looked at my assistant and I said, "What do we do now?"

He motioned toward the casino.

So, we took the big man and the dwarf down to the casino.

Bedlam broke out in the casino when we walk in the double doors. Everybody tried to figure out where the dwarf was going because that's where they wanted to be. We were going to the craps table because that's what we did, but they weren't sure yet. They would kind of move for the roulette table and then move for the poker tables. They would move around waiting for us to go somewhere. Finally, they decided we were going to the craps table: they mobbed the craps table, lining up four-, five-, six-deep around the craps table.

By the time we got to the craps table, the stick man already pulled up a stool for the dwarf. The big man put the dwarf up on the stool and the dwarf stood there.

The two dice went to the person shooting to the left of the dwarf, which meant dice would go in a clockwise rotation around the table. A shooter would roll the dice until that person seven-ed out. Then the next shooter took the dice. So, it was going to be a few minutes before the dwarf had an opportunity to exercise his magic.

After about the second shooter to his left, the dwarf, who was grouchy, said something that I couldn't understand.

The big man said, "He wants a cognac."

I held up my hand for and a waiter came over.

I said, "Bring the dwarf a cognac, please."

When the cognac arrives, he had to use two hands to hold the glass, but instead of sipping it, the dwarf just knocked it back.

The dice went three or four more people, and the dwarf said, "I want another cognac." Waiter brought another cognac. He knocked it back.

The dice went three or four more people and the dwarf said, "I want another cognac." Waiter brought yet another cognac, he knocked it back.

I was beginning to worry about the dwarf because he was getting a little wobbly on his stool. I was holding him on the knees so he wouldn't fall off the stool.

After maybe one or two more cognacs, the dice finally came around to the dwarf. By this time, he was drunk and rears back with the dice. He couldn't hold the dice in one hand because his hands were very small, so he used both hands. He shot at the end of the table, but the dice went high and hit a woman in the head. She started bleeding profusely from her nose. Immediately, some employees ran up to her with a napkin and stopped the blood flowing. They tried to take her to get First Aid, but she wouldn't go. She kept saying that she was not leaving the table. She had a prime front row seat.

Well, pesos were piling on the table. There were stacks at pesos in front of every shooter, plus the people behind them.

The dwarf rolled the dice and shot the dice. Everybody won. They applauded the dwarf, who got the dice and shot again. Everybody won again. He shot again—and everyone won yet again. People screaming and shouting for the dwarf.

The dwarf was hot and profitable. Our money was doubling every roll of the dice. This went on for at least half an hour.

All the sudden, he stopped shooting. He put the dice down, climbed off the stool like it was a ladder, and started for the door.

I turned to the big man and I said, "Where is the dwarf going?"

He said, "The dwarf is drunk, he is going home to bed."

I said, "Bring the dwarf back, he's got to finish rolling. He hasn't lost the dice yet."

He said, "The dwarf said he won't come."

I said, "Put the dwarf on the stool."

The dwarf crossed his arms in defiance and said, "I am not going to shoot the dice unless you promise I can make commercials for Señor Peynado, my friend."

I said, "Yes, you can make commercials, do whatever you want. Shoot the dice."

So, he brought the dwarf back and sat him up on a stool.

I said, "Now shoot!"

The dwarf nodded and hit two more numbers. He was still hot when he seven-ed out.

The big guy said, "Look, I got to take him and put him to bed."

He put the dwarf under his arm like a suitcase and carried him out of the casino.

We had several hundred American dollars in pesos by this time. We went to the Spanish restaurant as planned. We paid for everything in pesos.

Early the next morning the phone jangled. It was way too early for Dominicans, who are not early risers, and especially for somebody who had a lot of scotch and wine at the Spanish restaurant the night before.

I picked up the phone. It was Jacinto.

He said, "Raymond, did you tell my dwarf that he could make a TV commercial?"

I said, "Afraid I did."

He said, "Then you come get him because he's been here since the daylight to make his commercial. He's bothered my wife, my children, and everybody around here."

I said, "Send someone to get me."

Then I called a guy named Elias, who had a little television studio across town. Elias was still drunk from the night before. Dominicans are prodigious rum drinkers.

I told him to get his studio open, with a stool and a blue backdrop. I was bringing a dwarf to make a commercial.

He said, "Are you crazy, man?"

I said, "No, no, do this for me," because I had spent a lot of money with him.

He said, "Okay."

So, the men with the automatic weapons pick me up, along with the dwarf. We went to the studio and put the dwarf on a stool.

He said, "What do you want me to say?"

I said, "Say anything you want."

I said, "Action."

He liked that word and started talking. He talked for about five or six minutes in rapid Spanish. I understood about ten percent of what he was saying. Every now and then he would say "Jacinto, Jacinto, Jacinto."

The cameraman, who could understand the dwarf better than me, finally said, "I think the dwarf is finished."

I said, "Okay."

The dwarf looked at me and asked, "Is it good?"

I said, "Wonderful, just wonderful—couldn't do any better."

He got off the stool and the bodyguards took him home.

Elias said, "What do you want me to do with this?"

I said, "Nothing. Absolutely nothing—there's nothing we can do with it."

Jacinto and I went about our campaign.

Two or three days later Jacinto called and asked, "When is the dwarf's commercial going to run?"

I said, "It's never going to run. Sir, you know it's over five minutes long."

He said, "You got to do something with it. My dwarf and all his friends are driving me crazy."

I said, "Let me figure it out."

So, I went back to Elias and said, "Elias, make me a hundred VCR copies of that dwarf's monologue." I put the dwarf's picture on all hundred of them. Then I hired two other dwarves to go through the dwarf neighborhood, leaving the tapes on door stoops.

It turns out there is a huge neighborhood of dwarves in San Domingo. They spoke their own peculiar form of Spanish and were known as belligerent to outsiders. A normal-sized person could get stoned or attacked if they went into the neighborhood. For example, the government tried to build a fire substation in the dwarf neighborhood and the construction workers have been stoned so often it had been stopped. For years there had been a foundation sitting there with no fire station on top of it because the dwarves didn't want anybody in their neighborhood.

I would have needed more than a hundred copies for the entire neighborhood, but a hundred would do what I needed to do. The tapes seemed to please the dwarves for a while.

Luck was with Jacinto on Election Day and he won. Two years later, he called me and said, "Are you ready to do another campaign? I'm running for president. Balaguer is going to retire."

I said, "Sure."

So, I went down to Santo Domingo. I turned on the television set in my hotel room and saw something amazing.

Jacinto's dwarf had his own television show. He was standing on a stool with a big wizard hat and a wizard robe that went all the way down to the floor. He was making political predictions—he had become a political prognosticator. With the dwarf, of course, this was a magic show that people believed in. The dwarf had become a superstar.

Later, I was in a campaign meeting and there was going to be a big political parade. The locals said, "Does that sound good?"

I said, "Sounds good, except I don't know where the float is for the dwarves."

Well, when I went to the parade, there was a float filled with dwarves.

I learned to be careful of what I told anyone in the Dominican Republic.

Jacinto was not as lucky in his presidential campaign: he finished third on Election Day.*

---

*For an earlier version of this story, see Strother, *Falling Up*, 276–281.

II. Campaigns

Firing a Candidate

Jerry Austin

In 1984, I found a Democratic candidate running for Congress in Illinois's 19th Congressional District. His name was Terry Bruce and he was a Democratic state senator. His opponent in the general election was incumbent Republican Congressman Dan Crane. Crane was the brother of Illinois Congressman Phil Crane—the Jim Jordan of his time.

Many times, political consultants will take a race that is unwinnable, but will allow them to earn money. That's what this race was for me. Unfortunately, candidate Bruce would call me—leave messages to return his call—with crazy ideas for TV ads. As with most candidates, he couldn't count to thirty using a watch. And his ideas were goofy. The cardinal rule when running against the incumbent is that they have to be the issue, not you.

However, as it happens in life and in politics, luck came into this race.

Congressman Crane was accused of having had sex with a seventeen-year-old intern working in the House of Representatives. In response, Crane announced a series of press conferences throughout the district featuring his wife, mother, and children. I attended the first press conference in Champaign-Urbana, home of the University of Illinois. I did not have enough money to video the press conference and I did not have a tape recorder.

To my astonishment, Crane asked for forgiveness. He stated that his wife forgave him, his mother forgave him, and his children forgave him.

Bruce raised enough money to allow me to put the following spot on the air. And I previewed the ad for the local press, thereby earning media coverage before the ad was on TV.

I found an elderly woman. She had voted for Crane every time he had run. Sitting on her porch, she looked into the camera, and said, "Dan Crane, I've voted for you every time you've run for Congress. Your wife forgives you; your mother forgives you; and your children forgive you. And I forgive you. But I can't vote for you. I'm voting for Terry Bruce."

The response to the ad was better that I could have predicted. Except Terry Bruce had written another spot. I told him: the spot on the air was all that was necessary to win. He wanted to look in the camera and ask for the vote. I responded, "the old woman had done that and she was more credible than you."

He insisted I produce his ad. I refused. I didn't quit.

I fired him.

He never was able to get his spot on the air. But he won and was re-elected to three more terms. I lost income from three future congressional races.

But I had a great story.

Postscript

Is it plagiarism to plagiarize yourself?

In 1992, my firm represented State Senator Sanford Bishop in his run for the Democratic Party nomination in Georgia's 2nd Congressional District. His opponent, an incumbent, was six-term Congressman Charles Hatcher.

The chances of an African American beating an incumbent congressman from his own party was a long shot. But Hatcher had a problem: he was one of dozens of members of Congress involved in the check-writing scandal or "Rubber Gate." He had written over eight hundred checks on his House account and had not paid back a penny in almost three years.

Hatcher apologized and stated he would repay the amount due.

I suggested to my colleague, David Heller, who was handling the Bishop campaign for my firm, to consider my "I forgive you" ad. He asked me to come down to Columbus, Georgia, to shoot the ad with him. His job was to find an older woman who had always voted for Hatcher and he found an elderly white woman who was absolutely perfect.

The script was the same as against Crane without the reference to his family members who forgave him. She sat on a park bench, looked right into the camera, and delivered the familiar line perfectly: "I forgive you Charles, but I can't vote for you."

Bishop made history. Up until 2020, he was the only African American candidate to beat an incumbent congressman in a Democratic primary. Bishop continues to represent his district in the U.S. House and Heller continues to make his commercials.

Post Postscript

Is it plagiarism or reusing what had worked?

In 2008, I was asked to manage the re-election campaign of Congressman Steve Cohen in Memphis, Tennessee. Steve had won a multi-candidate primary in 2006 to replace Congressman Harold Ford, Jr., who was running for the U.S. Senate. With his victory, Cohen became the only white congressman to represent a majority African American district.

Cohen was challenged by an African American woman, Nikki Tinker, in the Democratic primary. She was a lawyer for a local airline and endorsed by Emily's List.

Was Cohen's voting record out of sync with his constituents' positions on issues? No. His one negative: he was white.

Tinker went on the air with a racist ad and then an antisemitic ad. Leaders in the minority—but in this district majority—community denounced her ads and her campaign.

Cohen had more support in the African American community than his 2006 primary victory revealed. He had been a state senator for over twenty years representing a district with a large African American population. Cohen was destined to win, but by what margin?

A week before the primary, I had a visitor at the campaign office. Her name was Mother Witt. I was unfamiliar with her since I wasn't from Memphis. She was a personality on African American radio with a very large local following.

She wanted to help Congressman Cohen. I asked if she would record a radio ad. She agreed. I asked her to meet me at the studio in an hour and I would have a script for her to review.

My first thought was to do a traditional endorsement. "This is Mother Witt. I am endorsing Congressman Steve Cohen because. . .."

Instead, my script was: "This is Mother Witt. You know me. I ask you to join me in forgiving Nikki Tinker for running a racist ad against Congressman Steve Cohen. Nikki Tinker, I forgive you for running an antisemitic ad against Congressman Steve Cohen. I forgive you Nikki Tinker, but I can't vote for you."

Cohen won the primary with almost eighty percent of the vote and has easily won every election since 2008.

He remains the only white congressman to represent a majority African American district.

Signs, Wires, Hats, Gloves — and a Jacket

Kevin Lampe

In the mid-1990s I was working on an insurgent congressional campaign. We were running against Phil Crane in Illinois' 8th Congressional District. Phil Crane was the longtime congressman, a conservative icon. Many people had run against him, but he always beat them.

Working on this race was one of my good friends, Patrick, who has since passed. A brilliant political operative, incredibly creative, and daring—but also with a heart of gold.

During the campaign, of course, we had no resources. We didn't have enough signs, and when we did get some signs, we didn't have money to get enough wire to put them up. But we noticed that Phil Crane's signs had great pieces of wire. They had two pieces of wire in each yard sign. We could use those pieces of wire for our yard signs.

Patrick has this great idea. He would call the Crane headquarters and ask them if he could get fifty signs to place around the district. Then he'd pick them up during the middle of the night because he worked second shift at the O'Hare airport. Could they leave them outside with the name "Sam" on them? They said, "Oh yeah, sure. We'll leave them out for you."

We didn't know if they would do that and so we went over around midnight in my pickup truck, which was formerly a Sears Pest Control truck. In the right light, you could still see where it said "Sears Pest Control" on it. We pulled up in my pickup truck, and lo and behold: there was a bunch of signs out there with a note saying, "Here's for you, Sam."

Terrific. We threw the signs in the back of the truck, took them back to the campaign office, shredded the Crane signs, put them in the recycling bin at a different shopping center, and then proceeded to use the wire for our yard signs. About a week later, Patrick called and said, "Hey, can I get some more signs? I think I'm going to use about seventy-five." They said, "Oh yeah, that'd be great, Sam. Go ahead."

Once again, we went over at midnight, picked up seventy-five signs and took them back to the campaign headquarters and used the wire for ourselves.

So, Patrick decides, "I'm going to try it one more time," and calls over and asks, "Can I get a hundred signs?" They said, "Yeah, and I tell you, Sam, you've been doing such a good job putting these signs up. We see them all over the district. We have a present for you."

All right, so we're kind of worried here. Are they setting us up? We took two cars. Patrick first drove around and noticed that the yard signs were out there. There was a jacket with the signs. Patrick looked at the jacket, embroidered with "Sam" on the front and on the back is a big "Crane for Congress" logo. Then, we pulled in with my truck, we threw the signs in the back, we take them, and use the wire.

Now, of course, the campaign ended in November. During the wintertime, Patrick would always carry a couple of dozen warm weather caps and pairs of gloves to give to homeless people. Once he had the jacket in the car, the next time he went on one of these wonderful night runs dropping off hats and gloves to the homeless people, he also dropped off the "Crane for Congress" jacket.

Mr. Ed Talks Again
David Heller

When I started as a media consultant working with Jerry Austin in 1992, one of our very first clients, Sanford Bishop, was an African American state senator running for Congress in southwest Georgia. Until 2020, Bishop was the only African American to beat a white incumbent in a Democratic primary for Congress. Two years later, Bishop easily won re-election to Congress.

In 1995, however, a 5–4 majority of the Supreme Court ruled that the redistricting of Georgia had violated the equal protection clause of the Fourteenth Amendment to the United States Constitution. The 2nd district was thus redrawn. The newly redrawn district went from majority African American to sixty percent white. Seeing opportunity, an old, crusty peanut farmer from Dawson, Georgia, named Wilbur Gamble, decided to run against Bishop in the 1996 Democratic primary—and polling showed the primary campaign to be closer than we would have hoped.

With money tight and a competitive general election looming in a presidential year, the Bishop campaign decided to run radio ads in the primary throughout southwest Georgia targeting older white voters. I thought it would be fun to use humor in the ads. It is a way to make the ads stand out and cut through the clutter of some crowded media markets. One of the first ads we aired was a spoof of the old TV show, "Mr. Ed."

If you remember that show, the only person the horse talks with was named Wilbur. So, I made a radio spot referencing Gamble's negative attacks on Congressman Bishop in which the horse says, "Wilbur, why are you saying these ugly things about Sanford Bishop?" The spot was funny—it won a Pollie award for best radio ad in a congressional campaign—and we could tell it was catching on with our targeted older voters.

In fact, Congressman Bishop had heard that the spot was driving Gamble nuts. So, one night, when Bishop and Gamble had a debate scheduled, I thought I would have some fun. I went into the auditorium and there were two podiums on the stage. The auditorium held a few hundred people. I found two young white kids and gave them each twenty bucks to run up to the stage and make a "neigh" sound like a horse, then mimic the horse's voice in the ad by saying, "Hey Wilbur!" and wave to him.

Just before the debate starts, the kids ran up to Gamble and deliver their lines perfectly. Gamble's face flashed red with anger; his hands white from gripping the podium so tight. He was furious. Congressman Bishop then strode on stage calm, cool, and collected. Bishop easily won the debate, then went on to win the primary by nearly twenty points. He continued on to win the general election and, in so doing, made the seat safe for himself. A decade-and-a-half later, Congressman Bishop is still serving the people of southwest Georgia with alacrity and aplomb.

The Louisiana Way of Doing Business
Bill Fletcher

Working in a modern political campaign is typically a mind-numbing, soul-sucking string of seemingly endless days. But not in Louisiana. About four-thirty or five p.m. every day, Louisiana people start asking, "Where we gonna go eat?" Campaign work continued with dinner, discussing strategy and the events of the day. If you're writing, you might take the work with you to the restaurant. Decisions get made. Money gets raised.

Eating at a relatively early hour means that sometimes you end up in the same restaurant with the consultants working for the other side. In 1991, I was a media consultant working for Edwin Edwards, who was trying to make a comeback for governor against Buddy Roemer. One night, I found myself in the same restaurant with Ray Strother, who was representing Roemer.

One of the things we had picked up in our focus groups was that people had come to hate Governor Roemer's voice. He had this sort of high-pitched, tinny voice and choppy delivery. A piercing, Southern, nasal twang. I thought Ray had figured out the same thing because in their campaign's first television spots Roemer did not speak. It is relatively unusual for a sitting governor not to be carrying his own message.

I had a couple martinis in me and Ray was drinking at the bar. So, I walked up to Ray and started digging him about the TV spots not having Roemer's voice. Ray was a revered figure in the business, especially in Louisiana. I'm just a punk kid from Tennessee. I knew I was way out over my skis.

Ray got a little defensive. He didn't know we had all of Roemer's old spots from four years before and that I had just finished making some spots for us that were almost one hundred percent Roemer's voice. Our spots were taking things he had said four years before that turned out to be not true, false, or whatever. The point was the people of the "Gret Stet of Loooisanna" were going to hear Roemer's voice.

I wrapped up my digs on Ray by saying, "Well, if you won't put Buddy's voice on TV, I'm going to." Our spots went up the next day.

One day early in the campaign Edwin Edwards asked me and Bill Morgan—my partner who had been Ray Strother's partner but was working with us for Edwards—over to his house. The invitation was highly unusual. He didn't ever want to meet with us.

Edwards asked, "Do you go eat at Ruth's Chris Steakhouse?"

We said, "Yes, sir. That's kind of where everybody goes."

Edwards said, "It's an embarrassment to me that you go there and that you don't buy my friends their dinner. So, from now on, anytime you go in there, and if you see my friends and you know who they are, you tell the waiter you'll pick up their dinner. And of course, I want you to turn the receipts into the campaign."

Well, the word got out, and then either Morgan or I had to be at Ruth's Chris Steakhouse every night. We were spending like two grand a night on steak dinners. It was perfectly aboveboard and there was nothing even remotely illegal about it.

However, most modern-day campaigns are eighteen-hour day affairs, with people eating at their desks and grabbing food when they can. Things are so relentlessly focused on efficiency and spending every dollar and measuring everything. So, if a media consultant starts turning two grand a night for whiskey and red meat, then you know some nerd's going to come and say, "This is going to end up costing us fifty grand!" You wouldn't be able to do it. But that was just the Louisiana way of doing business.

A lot of people forget that this race started out as a rematch between Democrats Buddy Roemer and Edwin Edwards in the primary. Things didn't change much when Roemer shocked everyone by switching to the Republican Party early in the campaign. The campaign only became a race between Edwards and Republican David Duke, a former leader of the Ku Klux Klan, in the run-off.

In all our polling, Edwards was always at about thirty-five percent. The words people used to describe Edwards were "crook, crooked, and corrupt." We did all the normal and customary things one would do inside of a campaign, make TV commercials, raise money, and whatnot. But we just stayed at thirty-five percent no matter what, no matter how good or bad the TV commercials were, how much more or less we spent or how many fish fries, crawfish boils, or steak dinners we sponsored.

We were stuck at thirty-five percent in a three-way race—which was bad for us. We needed to be in a runoff with Duke, that was the only way that Edwards could become governor. If we went into a runoff with Roemer, it wouldn't happen.

We noticed that when Roemer came up in the polls, Duke went down. When Duke came up, Roemer came down. All the movement was with the other two candidates. Then something happened that is commonplace today but that was unheard of in 1991: An oil executive named Jack Kent spent about $600,000 on independent expenditures against Roemer, with about two and a half weeks to go before election day. It crashed Roemer and there we were in a runoff with David Duke.

Our first run-off polling came back, and it was forty percent for Edwards to forty percent for Duke, with twenty percent undecided. So, it was not a cakewalk.

This race presaged the Trump phenomenon we're seeing today. There was economic distress and somebody had to be blamed for it. Duke had gotten himself elected to the legislature in that white-flight district by talking about these issues, white empowerment, white victimhood, etc., etc., etc. Duke had also swiped right on the Karmic Tinder app and converted himself to Christianity. He told the people of Louisiana he was washed in the blood of the lamb and, thus, was forgiven of all his sins, including being a Nazi and a Ku Klux Klanner.

Once again, we weren't making very much progress in the polls. The KKK stuff against Duke wasn't working because it was all baked in the cake, everybody knew about it, and it wasn't considered news. Plus in a deeply religious state like Louisiana … hard-ankle Baptists in the rural areas, devoted Catholics down south, and African American churches of all stripes dominating the cities … people believed in the power of redemption. If they had been forgiven and redeemed, why not David Duke?

Case in point: In one focus group, a man wearing a camouflage hunting hat declared he could never vote for someone who had avoided the draft. We then presented evidence to him and the rest of the group showing that Duke had obviously avoided the Vietnam-era draft. Without missing a beat, the man leaned back, crossed his arms and said, "Vietnam. That was a bad war."

Edwin didn't believe in polling, but he loved a good one liner and delivered them constantly. In a speech during the primary, he said, "I built the interstate system in this state and Buddy Roemer can't cut the grass around it." In a small gaggle of reporters after a debate, Edwards advised the gathered reporters, "People should vote for me because I'm a wizard under the sheets, too."

The famous "Vote for the Crook. It's Important" bumper sticker was widely distributed. Edwin found it amusing. It was topped, in my opinion, by a handmade sign built by the same cinematographer who shot our television spot that said, "Vote Edwards. He's no Saint. But He's no Nazi."

We had to commission polls through the Democratic Party and outside groups. Mark Mellman came in with a poll for us through an outside group. He said that the race had become event-driven: an event would happen and people will rush over to Edwards, and then another event would happen and they would rush over to Duke.

It was back and forth, back and forth. Mark's advice to us, which was really good, was to make sure we had the last event, whatever it was.

Mellman and Morgan determined that an economic message would work where the anti-Nazi and Klan messages were failing: Duke as governor would hurt the Louisiana economy and run jobs out of the state.

So, for the last event of the campaign, we got approval to make a thirty-minute program.* We bought thirty-minute blocks of time in prime time on every television station in the state. Not cable, not access—we pre-empted network programs and bought time on broadcast television. We put about six or seven hundred points of thirty-second spots on the week leading up to the big program, even before I had the program finished, with teasers of the content to get free media as well.

We shot video in seven cities in one day. We interviewed private sector leaders about the economic consequences of electing David Duke. The CEO of Freeport-Mc-MoRan, the mining and drilling company that was the largest employer in the state at the time, said, "We left South Africa, we'll leave Louisiana." A producer for Disney came on camera and said, "I've talked to people at Disney and if David Duke becomes governor, they will not make another movie here." At the time, Disney was a big studio and made a lot of movies in New Orleans. We had Tom Benson, owner of the New Orleans Saints, say, "I love Louisiana, and I wanna stay in Louisiana, but if David Duke is governor, we'll have to consider taking the Saints somewhere else."

We also interviewed real people about their fear losing their jobs. With one crew using a small plane and the other in a production van, we gathered this crashing cavalcade of big organizations and little people saying, "Duke winning is going to hurt us."

I made the thirty-minute program at a studio in Baton Rouge. I had two edit suites going and I stayed up for fifty-six hours straight editing together this

---

*Ray Strother also considered a thirty-minute program in the race, see Strother, *Falling Up*, 255-256.

thirty-minute program in three parts. Finally, on the day we had to deliver it, we put it all together. Our delivery was supposed to be twenty-nine minutes and thirty seconds long, but we had twenty-eight minutes and fifty-nine seconds. So, I slapped a thirty-second commercial on the end of it and off it goes.

It was called "The Decision of Our Lives." There was one little side hit on the KKK in the middle of the thirty-minute program, but for the most part it was all about economics. We completely reoriented the argument to the economy, right at the end of the campaign. It had a tremendous impact.

Edwards won in a landslide.

There is a mostly forgotten fact that, thirty years before the Trump era of racial division, chillingly anticipates the current election dynamic: Six of every ten whites voted for David Duke. It was the African American and Cajun populations that swamped the Klansman. On election day, African American and Cajun radio stations gave traffic reports to let voters know how long lines were at voting stations. Black churches hauled thousands of voters to the polls. It was a beautiful thing to see, but it was nothing that the campaign had orchestrated or planned. The African American tidal wave of voting was almost completely organic.

The Best $300 I Ever Spent

Kitty Kurth

When Paul Tsongas ran for the Democratic presidential nomination in 1992, he had a tough uphill battle. The improbable campaign was becoming a bit more possible, however, after Tsongas won the New Hampshire primary. The campaign grew and attracted heavy hitters to our effort, like legendary Boston advance man Jim King, and Jerry Austin, the media consultant who had transformed Jesse Jackson's 1988 presidential run from a grassroots effort to legitimate contender status.

The Tsongas campaign in Illinois was a constant quest for miracles. Early on, I don't think that the boys in Boston believed that Paul would still be in the race after Super Tuesday, much less two weeks later for the Illinois primary.

In November, I got a call. Could I please organize the delegate recruitment and petition drive that was due mid-December to get us on the ballot? We had no staff in Illinois, no endorsements, and no money. What we did have was about three weeks to recruit delegates, print ballots, and gather twenty-five thousand signatures.

I still don't remember exactly how we did it. (I think it was kind of like childbirth—they say you forget how much it hurts or you would never do it again.) It was truly an impossible task, but I did not want to disappoint Paul Tsongas. So, we did it. By some miracle, somehow, we got the signatures—after calling every Illinois Democrat I had ever met and asking for help, And I got my first gray hair.

As I said, we did not have a lot of money, we did not have a lot of staff, and we did not have a lot of hope. But we had lots of volunteers. And we had Greeks. I figured if we had Greeks supporting us, maybe we could feed the volunteers.

I put one of the volunteers in charge of rounding up the Greek restaurant owners and putting together a schedule for donated meals. The Greeks were happy to oblige. In fact, it got to be quite competitive. They served us breakfast, lunch, and dinner— each meal was better than the last. I ate better the winter of 1992 than ever before or since. The volunteers were fed and happy. Another miracle.

In Illinois, our presidential primary lines up with St. Patrick's Day season. I say "season" because in Chicago, we make St. Patrick's Day last for several days. We even have two parades on two different days. And we dye the river green.

All the campaigns knew how much was at stake in the upcoming primary. We needed good press stories and time on TV was essential. Paul Tsongas was going to march in the South Side St. Patrick's Day parade to get some of that media attention.

A few days before, the advance man in charge of efforts for our part of the parade, Steve Graham, told me he needed $300 in cash. I was torn: first, we did not have a lot of money, and second, I did not know how we were going to record it on official filings. I was especially nervous when I asked him what the money was for, and he said, "You don't want to know."

I gave him the money and tried to forget about it.

Typically, the candidate marches in the parade and the campaign has to figure out how to arrange for the hundred or so members of the national press corps to get the best pictures and stories from along the parade route.

I made sure that our press people rode in a custom-made stake-bed truck. The truck gave the media a good vantage point high above the crowd. It was very sturdy, comfortable, and stable to allow for good pictures to be taken. Stocked with some home-made Irish soda bread and hot "coffee," it made for happy reporters.

The Clinton campaign took a different approach for their press operation. They thought it would look cool to have police horses for the parade. Basically, this involved herding the press corps inside a moving rope pen. While police horses might look cool, the way they had arranged it—horses ringing the outside, reporters in the middle—meant that the national press walked the long, chilly campaign route for hours, getting bumped and blocked in by police horses, not to mention walking in horse shit.

Guess which group of reporters got prettier pictures?

As Tsongas walked the two miles along the Western Avenue parade route, crowds cheered and Tsongas ran from side to side across the road greeting well-wishers. One of the photographers snapped a picture of Paul jumping two feet in the air in the parade revelry. It was a magical moment. After the parade, Paul told me that it was the first day he ever felt like he could really be elected president. Our third miracle.

Clinton himself had been booed by the Western Avenue bar patrons, while Tsongas was cheered and revered. The newspapers the next day had gloomy, complaining coverage of the Clinton campaign. The Tsongas coverage was glowing.

Later I found out that Graham had visited all of the taverns along Western Avenue and used his natural Boston Irish gift of gab to persuade them to hang Paul Tsongas banners along the parade route. It may have helped that while Graham had been bartering with the bar management to ask them to hang our banners, he was also careful to buy a few rounds for the regular patrons of the bars.

It was the best $300 I have ever spent on a campaign.

Candidates Say the Darndest Things
Garry South

When I was growing up, radio and TV personality Art Linkletter hosted a program called, *Kids Say the Darndest Things*, in which he would ask young children simple questions and let them respond in their own hilarious ways.

Political candidates aren't kids and should have developed the sort of filters that children often lack, but they still sometimes say stupid things—whether from being tired, distracted, confused, or for reasons that are downright inexplicable. And even the smartest candidates are not exempt, making faux pas or verbal mistakes, mispronouncing words. Remember when Barack Obama said during the 2008 presidential campaign for president that he had visited "all fifty-seven states"? Or referred in Iowa to "Whole Foods" stores—in a state that doesn't have any such stores? And who can forget Mitt Romney's "binders full of women" from the 2012 campaign debates?

Once of the funniest and most embarrassing politician gaffes I ever witnessed in person was committed by Richard Nixon, the first president I ever saw in the flesh, when I was in college in Montana in the 1970s. Nixon had come to the state to boost the candidacy of a Republican running for Congress. On the platform with him was former Representative Orvin Fjare, who had served in Congress in the 1950s when Nixon was vice president. Fjare's name was actually pronounced "fee-are'-ee," Anyway, after going on and on about how close a personal friend he was to "someone who is on this stage with me today" and how closely they had worked together when the person was in Congress, Nixon then said, "So I want you to give a big Montana welcome to Orvin Eff-jar!"

During my forty-plus years of working on campaigns at all levels, I have heard and seen candidates say things that are hilariously funny, and in some cases, unfathomably dumb. To spare them embarrassment, I will not name them, but here are a few of my favorites:

One candidate kept saying, "Unlike my opponent, I don't have a $1,000 Rolodex watch!"

Another candidate once referred to "the Apostle St. Paul's Epistle to the Philippines."

Keeping on the religion theme, a candidate who had been raised Episcopalian kept saying "Episcolopian."

A candidate in California several times referred to "more HIV lanes" as the answer to traffic congestion on the freeways.

When I asked another candidate who he was talking about when he several times referred to "the great Jewish NBA stars," he replied, "You know, guys like Julius Irving, Moses Malone, and Isaiah Thomas."

And not to be outdone, one opponent kept referring to my candidate as a "vegetarian," when he meant "veterinarian."

Another one kept confusing the NCAA with the NAACP.

So, see, candidates are just people, too—I think.

The NAACP Tournament

Garry South

In 1982, I wrote and produced radio spots for a Democratic candidate running for county executive of Prince George's County, Maryland. Parris Glendening was a professor of government and politics at the University of Maryland in College Park—and it showed. Although he had been elected previously to the Hyattsville Town Council and was in his second term on the Prince George's County Council, his demeanor was still quite stiff, very professorial and pedantic. Glendening was obviously smart. At the time, he was the youngest person in the history of Florida State University to have been awarded a doctorate. But his dry, slow, and somewhat belabored manner of speaking was, well, the opposite of riveting or exciting.

Prince George's County, adjacent to and northeast of Washington D.C., was then a largely blue-collar area, unlike the upscale Montgomery County, its Maryland neighbor to the west. Some of us in the campaign decided we really needed to try to loosen up Glendening somehow. While noodling on this objective, I hit on the bright idea of schlepping him around to some working-class sports bars in the county so he could observe real people and learn how to be more of a "regular guy."

This happened to be during the NCAA March Madness and lots of sports bars had their wall-mounted TVs tuned to the playoff games. Not a particular sports fan, we briefed Glendening pretty extensively on the mechanics and brackets of the NCAA playoffs before we launched the visits to the sports bars.

The first one we went into, there were some blue-collar-looking guys sitting at the bar watching one of the games. We nudged the candidate into approaching these men and introducing himself. He did, but then put his hand on the shoulder of one of them, with a tattoo on his arm, and blurted out, "So, what do think of this NAACP tournament?"

Cover blown!

The lesson I learned yet again was that you can only do so much to change a candidate's basic persona—I have often stated it in terms of "you can't make a chicken bark." But Glendening went on not only to win the county executive race, but served three terms in that position, and then was elected to two terms as governor of Maryland. So, his boring, scholarly manner obviously wasn't a career-ending trait.

American Joe
David Heller

In 1982, I worked for a little-known state senator from East Baltimore, "American Joe" Miedusiewski, who ran in the Democratic primary for county executive of Prince George's County, Maryland. There were seven candidates and American Joe was polling seventh. In fact, he polled at less than one percent when the campaign started. This fact wasn't surprising given the heavyweights in the race, including Parris Glendening, then the chair of the county council and a future governor of the state. He was the front-runner in the crowded field.

Prince George's County had a commissioner style of government, where each member of the county council served as the liaison to a department of county government. Glendening was the liaison for the police. He was constantly pumping himself up talking about crime. He said, "I've been out there on the front lines trying to fight crime because I'm a police commissioner." Yes, that's what he called himself, "police commissioner."

So, American Joe holds a press conference and calls Glendening out, "You're not a police commissioner, you disrespect every law enforcement officer when you call yourself the police commissioner."

Glendening, like an idiot, responds by saying, "I too am a police commissioner. In fact, I even have a badge and carry a gun!"

I turned to American Joe and said, "Just like Barney Fife," the deputy sheriff from the *Andy Griffith Show*. So, we put out an ad and had a press conference comparing Parris Glendening to Barney Fife. We shot up in the polls, and by the end of the race, we were in second place against Glendening.

But it wasn't enough: Glendening's bigger war chest allowed him to win.

Radon Ramble

Jack Corrigan

Before the 1988 Iowa caucuses, there was a debate on environmental issues in Cedar Rapids. Among the Democratic presidential candidates, Al Gore was very knowledgeable about the environment, and he wanted to demonstrate his expertise by catching his main target at that time, Dick Gephardt, off-guard.

During candidate-to-candidate questions, Gore posed a question to Gephardt. He asked, "Dick, I know you know radon is a very serious environmental threat, and like me, you have spent a lot of time thinking about radon and ways to deal with it. What is your policy for dealing with radon?"

Gephardt, whose face did not change at all while Gore asked the question, says, "You know Senator, I'm really glad you asked that question because I share your concern that radon is one of the most significant issues that we have to deal with. I think it's a very challenging issue and the way I think we ought to deal with it is to put together a group, a bicameral group, someone from the Senate, someone from the House, Democrats and Republicans, and see if we can build a consensus."

In the middle of this rambling two-minute response from Gephardt, Jesse Jackson turns to Mike Dukakis and quietly asks, "What the f*** is radon?"

Dukakis replied, "I don't know and neither does Dick."

Debating the Debate

Donald R. Sweitzer

In March of 1992, ABC News sponsored a debate in Dallas, Texas with the remaining Democratic presidential candidates at that time: Jerry Brown, Bill Clinton, Tom Harkin, and Paul Tsongas. The format of the debate was to be the four candidates sitting at a table with moderator Peter Jennings. There would be questions posed by Jennings to a candidate and the other candidates would have the ability to challenge the answer in a direct exchange.

The evening of the debate I accompanied Senator Harkin to the TV studio. James Carville was with Governor Clinton and Jerry Austin with Senator Tsongas. I can't recall who was with Governor Brown. Our candidates were in the makeup room sitting four across in a barbershop-like setting. We were in the greenroom where we would watch the debate.

About thirty minutes before the debate was to start, the candidates were told that ABC was changing the format. Instead of allowing the candidates to respond to each other's answers, ABC said that questions would be posed to a candidate by Peter Jennings with no opportunity for the others to challenge the answer.

Austin, Carville, and I rushed into the makeup room. Our three candidates did not want the new format. They were all angry. My recollection is that Jerry Brown was fine with it. The three of us had the same immediate reaction, which was "screw

ABC." We told our candidates that they should refuse to go on the air. Like all presidential debates, ABC had hyped this program for weeks beforehand and it was in prime time. We got an "Ok" from our candidates to go to ABC to tell them we were leaving. Brown, as usual, wouldn't play.

The three of us told someone from ABC that our candidates would not go on. My memory and Jerry Austin's memory of what came next is slightly different as to the setting. My recollection is that we came around a hallway corner, when we saw Roone Arledge, the president of ABC News, and Peter Jennings. Jerry recalls that we were in a closet off the hallway plotting our strategy when Arledge and Jennings came looking for us in a rage. Jerry's memory is probably more accurate than mine since I clearly remember that, wherever we were, it was dark.

I had never met Arledge. Arledge was riding pretty high and had become quite the well-known celebrity when he went from running ABC Sports to taking over ABC News. And Jennings, of course, was known worldwide as the longtime anchor of *ABC Nightly News*. I had met Jennings in the past but he really didn't know me.

We had a young embedded reporter with us on the Harkin campaign from ABC, Juju Chang. She was fresh out of college and very bright. She idolized Peter Jennings. I used to tease her on the campaign trail about how Jennings was a snob and not an American (Jennings was Canadian). She hated it when I did it, so, of course, I did it all the time.

We told Arledge and Jennings that the new format was unacceptable. My lasting memory of that moment was that they looked at each other and laughed. Jennings was leaning up against the wall with one leg against it. He was as smug as I imagined. Arledge was immediately combative. We told them that our candidates would refuse to go onstage. It was fifteen minutes before the red light would go on. They both laughed and said there was nothing we could do about it. It was their network and they were in control. They dared us to take our guys out.

At this point, I totally blew up. They were so condescending, looking at each other and rolling their eyes. That went right up my rear end. I lost it. I got right in Arledge's face and told him we were leaving. I turned to Jennings and started cursing him out for being such an arrogant ass. Austin and Carville were no shrinking violets: they both added their own well-honed intimidating qualities to the discussion. It probably only lasted about two or three minutes—I was in a rage. They really struck a nerve somewhere in me.

At about that time they realized we weren't fooling around.

We came back into the makeup room and told our candidates to freshen their makeup because ABC backed off and we were going back to the original format. What I loved about the three candidates was that they each had balls and were totally willing to walk out. Jerry, James, and I were very pleased with ourselves.

Everyone gathered at the hotel that night. In a presidential campaign everyone, campaign staff, print reporters, media people—and sometimes even the candidates—gather at hotel bars after big events. That's where reporters get their best stories. They have credit cards and always do the buying.

I found our ABC embed Juju, and had a great time telling her what a complete jerk Peter Jennings was. I reminded her of it every time I ran into her for years to come. I stopped when Jennings passed away. Juju went on to become an ABC reporter, did a stint on *Good Morning America*, and eventually hosted *Nightline*.

A Question of Timing

Jerry Austin

In 2006, I was the consultant to John Stroger, president of the Cook County Board of Commissioners. It was only second to the Los Angeles County Board of Supervisors in terms of power. I had helped elect Stroger in 1994. He was the first African American candidate to be elected to this office. After three terms, he was planning to retire. But before he announced his decision, Forest Claypool, an elected board member, and a David Axelrod client, announced he would challenge Stroger in the Democratic primary.

Stroger was pissed. He always planned to retire and support his son Todd as his replacement. He decided to run for one more term.

A few weeks before the primary election our advisory committee met before the weekly County Board meeting. Our research director told the group he uncovered a number of negatives regarding Claypool to be used in the campaign. Stroger laughed in response. He left to conduct the board meeting, which was televised live. None of the campaigns staff watched the televised meeting because it was recorded.

Later that morning the woman responsible for the taping asked if I heard what happened at the meeting. I said, "No," but I was on my way to the County building to view the tape.

Stroger had called the meeting to order and began to call the roll of board members. He said "Forest Claypool," who responded "Present." Instead of calling the next name, Stroger said, "Forest Claypool, we have a bunch of negatives on you."

Claypool exclaimed, "Be specific. Be specific."

Stroger just laughed.

When others on the campaign team viewed the tape, they thought we had a problem. They envisioned Axelrod creating a spot where negatives on Stroger would be aired and they'd have Stroger laughing in response.

I had a better idea. I quickly produced an ad starting with Claypool challenging, "Be specific." After this exclamation, the voice over would say, "Ok, Forest, I'll be specific," and listed one of his negatives. I think we were able to answer "Be specific" four times in the thirty-second ad. I started airing the spot ten days before the primary.

One week before the primary, Stroger had a heart attack. David Axelrod said he'd never been in a campaign where the opponent has a heart attack the week before the election. He suspended all Claypool election activities out of respect for Mr. Stroger.

But I didn't suspend our election activities. The "Be Specific" ad stayed on the air through primary day.

Stroger won the primary by eight percentage points. He was the Democratic Party nominee. The primary was in March. It was obvious the Stroger was very sick and probably wouldn't be alive in November. The party leaders started pressuring Stroger to resign as the nominee in favor of someone younger whom they would appoint to replace him. He refused. He said he would only resign if they appointed his son Todd as the party nominee. The party leaders refused initially. They saw Todd as a lightweight who took advantage of his father's name to be elected to the Cook County Board. But after a period of time, the party leaders agreed to appoint Todd. He became the nominee and barely won in November against a weak Republican candidate. He served four years and was beaten in the 2010 primary.

John Stroger died in 2008, living to see his son elected to succeed him and passing before he was defeated.

Money, Mistakes, and Timing
Joe Slade White

According to a friend, I supposedly once said: "Never mistake having a lot of money for being good."

That's good, I guess, because I haven't had that many campaigns that have had "a lot of money." "A lot of money" could be defined as "money to burn."

I work for Democrats—and not the few billionaire Democrats who exist. Over the decades, I've worked mostly for the men and women who've had to scrape to put together enough money to pull off an upset. Sometimes that can be enormous fun. I usually joke that if I'm *very*, very good in this life, I get to come back as a Republican consultant. But *not* having too much money can actually be a good thing when it comes to winning upset campaigns.

Republicans are sort of like the British Redcoats back in the Revolutionary War. They have the best muskets, the best boots, the best uniforms, and they march into battle in lines so straight they'd make a drill sergeant weep. Whatever they want, they can buy it. Whatever they want to try to do, they can afford it. They believe they can do everything. It's impressive—and wrong.

When a campaign tries to do everything, some things will go wrong, and some will go wrong badly and irreversibly so. Campaigns make mistakes. Often a campaign won't realize it, because after all, they just spent a lot of money on those things.

But every campaign makes mistakes. Every day—some important, some so small that no one pays a price or loses their job.

When you have a campaign that is starving for money, but that maybe just maybe will have enough, you realize you can't do everything. In fact, you can't do very many things. You have to choose carefully. Almost always that means breaking some long-held rules that people will tell you can't be tampered with. Sometimes you beat the Redcoats with their shiny new muskets, because your ragtag rebel army is shooting from behind the rocks and the trees and not marching in straight lines.

When you don't have a lot of money—when you have just barely enough—you figure out what you can do well, and you figure out exactly when you can do it, which is always later than anyone who's following the rule book tells you. Without a lot of money, you are less tempted to do something early, badly, and showing your hand before you should.

Because you're doing fewer things, you know you have to do them right. You aren't diverted by too many things happening at once (especially when a couple of those things start going bad on you). That doesn't mean that every consultant or every campaign without a lot of money wins. There is incompetence operating at all levels of campaigns. But I don't mind having to be careful—having to scope things out—to play out lots of scenarios, so that I can be three or four moves ahead on the campaign chess board.

In one campaign for governor in an industrial state, our opponent was a multi-billionaire businessman (do you remember when we didn't have to put "multi" in front of "billionaire"? When billionaire alone was enough to convey just how stupidly rich someone was?) This Republican billionaire and his Republican consultants decided that it would be a good (and for them an affordable) idea to go on the air with saturation buys starting in February. Millions of dollars in television buys. Even the family dog couldn't wander through the living room without seeing one of their ads. They were saturation bombing the voters.

Conventional wisdom says you cannot remain off the air for very long when an opponent goes on the air. The problem was, there was no way to go up on the air that early without running out of money halfway through the campaign. That's what our opponent wanted us to do (and it's almost never a good idea to do what your opponent wants you to do). Plus, we would have been fighting on his ground, his terms, defensively—also a losing proposition.

So, the chief consultant for the campaign wisely said, "Okay. We're going to go down into the fall-out shelter, into the storm cellar, into the bunker, and we're going to close that steel door behind us. We're not going to think about what's going on above ground. What we are going to do is figure out the minimum we can raise realistically. And we're going to plan a campaign for that budget. Once we get that amount of money or if we fall below a certain number in our own polling, we go on the air. Not before."

Party insiders thought we were nuts. Of course they did. Our opponents wondered what the hell we were up to.

So, we waited and we waited, and after five months had past, we were at our goal of just enough money to run our campaign well.

Everyone knew what our opponent's chief vulnerability was. He had fired over a thousand people in the state and then spent millions to build factories in China where things could be manufactured more cheaply.

One of the chief problems with billionaire business people is that they can't understand how a good business decision can ever be thought of as bad. And the decision our opponent made was a good business decision for his stockholders (mainly his family). In fact, I'm pretty sure, throughout the rest of the campaign, our opponent never came to grips with how a business move as smart as this one could hurt him. It's how smart business people think. Especially if they are billionaires surrounded by people who tell them how brilliant they are twenty-four hours a day.

The opponent's consultants were absolutely sure and had convinced themselves that we would lead off with attack ads on the issue of firing a thousand local people and shipping their jobs overseas. It made sense.

But in campaigns timing is everything—not possibly everything, not very important—*It's everything*. Waiting to make the right move (and it's almost always later than anyone thinks is wise) is everything in winning an upset campaign, when you're being outspent and are going against the odds.

When we did go up with TV ads in the summer, they weren't attack ads at all. I knew we needed to get our job performance numbers up—not skyrocketing—but up out of the hole. Slowly and surely, the ads were quiet and factual, and probably as close to being the opposite of exciting as I could make them. Again, the party experts thought we were nuts (or at least that I was nuts). After all, the monster was at the door—kill the monster!

The opponent's consultants were also perplexed. They were on the edge of their seats anticipating a barrage of negative ads. I even helped this along by titling the ads with names like "One Thousand Jobs," "Real People Laid Off," and "Factories in China," knowing that once any of our ads were delivered to the stations our opponents would be alerted to the title of the ads, and would run around in circles, waving their arms.

Our positive numbers on job performance started inching up. We would need the rest of the campaign to get them into non-radioactive levels, but the start had been made. It was important to get it done early. And it was vital to get it done in a way that would be credible—not flashy or reactive.

Then right after Labor Day, we launched our first ad about firing those people, shipping their jobs overseas, and investing millions in building factories in China. Now voters were paying attention. Now we were giving them a good show to watch: David versus Goliath. And we'd picked up the right pebbles for the sling shot. Our opponent's numbers started to slide—not free fall—but sliding. As any mountain climber will tell you, a slide on a slope will always accelerate and if not stopped quickly the outcome of a slide like that is almost always fatal.

In the end our candidate won. This was a race no one in Washington D.C. thought could be won. (This was another advantage because that meant Washington D.C. left us alone and didn't interfere.) We were outspent by an absurd $27 million. We should have lost. Yet *not* having a lot of money forced us to think things through. Our "disadvantage" forced us to come up with new rules as fast as we were breaking the old ones.

And yes, we did have enough money. Campaigns that don't have enough money generally lose. Having enough money is what it takes to give an underdog campaign a chance to win. And as always, timing was everything. As Matt Damon playing Carroll Shelby said in the movie *Ford vs. Ferrari*, "Wait for it. Wait for it. Now!"

Fired on the Spot

David Heller

Everyone likes to talk about a race they won. I'll tell you about a race that didn't work out.

In 2000, I was working for a multi-millionaire running for Congress in West Virginia named Jim Humphreys. Humphreys was a long shot running against a well-liked Secretary of State. I had written a flight of spots. The whole theme was Humphreys was a trial lawyer who beat the insurance companies in court, so he'll beat them for you in Congress. Rather than have the Republicans wrap his professions around his neck in the fall, I wanted to embrace it early on.

So, I write three scripts for TV and there are three spots. We film the first two and the third featured a senior citizen talking about how Jim Humphreys would stand up for her on Medicare and Social Security. The campaign finds a senior citizen that will go on camera. The senior lives in a nursing home. We go to the nursing home and set up the shoot.

All of the sudden there is a problem.

"Dave, you got to come over here."

"What's the problem?"

"She won't do it."

"What do you mean she won't do it?"

"The lights, the camera, it's too intimidating. She doesn't want to be on television, she won't do it."

"Can we get someone to persuade her to do it?"

"No, she's set in her mind, she won't do it."

Humphreys said, "What are we going to do?"

"Well, you got two choices," I said. "You can find someone else, or we can come back another day, and film it then. But that's going to be expensive for you to bring a camera crew to West Virginia."

Humphreys said, "Well, let's see if we can find somebody else."

So, we start going through the nursing home looking for someone who will do it. I find this elder woman, and she says, "I'm a Democrat, I'd love to do it for you!"

"Really?"

"Oh, yeah!"

"How old are you?"

"Ninety-five years young!"

I show her the script, she reads it, and said, "I'm happy to say this, it will be no problem at all."

I introduce her to Humphreys and he thanks her for doing the spot.

She said, "You're a Democrat? You're going to protect Medicare and Social Security? That's great. I'm happy to help you."

We light the scene, put her in there, get her a little bit of makeup, and she was as good an on-camera spokesperson as I have seen in my life. She goes in, reads the script, and like a professional actress, nails it. Two takes, three takes, no problem—she was perfect.

I produce all three spots. Humphreys sees the spots and loves them. The campaign loves the spots. The spots go up on the air. We are moving up in the polls, the campaign has momentum. We put up her spot and people start telling Humphrey what a great spot it is. We are closing the gap.

Then the campaign gets a phone call from the elderly woman's daughter demanding we pull the spot.

"What do you mean we have to pull the spot?" I said, "I have a signed permission slip."

It turns out that the elderly woman had Alzheimer's disease. She had no idea what she was doing. She does this press conference and rips on Humphreys for the spot.

Humphreys responds the only way a courageous politician could: "I had no idea what was going on. My media consultant is fired!"

I was fired on the spot.

As Luck Would Have It

Jerry Austin

In campaigns, as in life, luck plays a role. You don't know if it's going to be good luck or bad luck, you just hope to have more good luck than bad luck. During a campaign, bad luck really can be devastating, while good luck is exhilarating.

This story is about bad luck and good luck both happening simultaneously.

Dick Celeste was running for Ohio governor in 1982. He had been the director of the Peace Corps during the Carter administration. We were touting his management experience.

Bad luck: During the primary campaign, the General Accounting Office (GAO) put out a ten-year study of the Peace Corps. In that study, there was criticism of how the agency was managed. The study never mentioned anyone's name as being responsible, and Dick had been the director for less than two years, but one of our opponents put out a radio spot questioning Dick's management experience based on the GAO report.

Dick's wife called me and said we had to do a spot in response. They wanted to put Sargent Shriver, the original director of the Peace Corps, on TV saying what a great job Dick Celeste did managing the agency.

She and Dick had written a spot. I'm always *thrilled* when candidates write spots. I met them at the campaign office that same night. The spot they wrote was two minutes and thirty-four seconds—that's two minutes and four seconds too long. I told them their ad does not work.

What are we going to do, they asked?

Good luck: The same day as our opponent's radio ad, a young woman came into the Columbus campaign office to volunteer. The coordinator greeted her, thanked her for offering to volunteer, asked who she was and where she lived. She was a graduate student at Ohio State and a former Peace Corps volunteer. She served while Dick was the director.

In addition, she described how she was kidnapped by Sandinista guerrillas. She showed the coordinator a copy of a local Spanish newspaper exhibiting a picture of her surrounded by Sandinistas wearing bandanas. She said Celeste had secured her release.

The coordinator called me and told me the above story. I instructed him to ask the young woman if she would record a TV spot telling her story. Would she state that Director Celeste saved her life?

She agreed to record the spot, but she wouldn't say Celeste "saved my life." She did say, "If it wasn't for Director Celeste, there's a good chance I would not be here today."

The ad was put on the air immediately. We went up five points.

You're Running Against Whom?

Tony Fazio

Carmel is a picturesque little city on the Monterey Peninsula off the coast of California. It is not usually a hotbed of political activity. It came as a complete surprise when I got a call from Mayor Charlotte Townsend. She wanted some help with her re-election campaign.

I thought to myself, "How hard can this be? I might even be able to get to know the mayor and take my wife there for a much-needed weekend vacation."

I launched into my usual questions to find out what the demographics were like, what the major's issues were, how long she had been the mayor—the usual stuff.

She was the Democrat in the race, and since we only did Democrats, I did not think it was necessary to ask her right away about her opponent. It probably was some disgruntled developer who wanted to do something egregious to this lovely sleepy little village that its residents would not tolerate anyway.

As our conversation progressed and I got to get to know her better, I started to notice some hesitation in her voice.

So, I finally asked her the question, "By the way, who is your opponent?"

She said with some trepidation, and with some sigh of relief that she finally got to the big reveal, "My opponent is Clint Eastwood."

Silence ensued while I regained my composure.

I said, "You're running against whom?"

Maybe there was some other person with the same name, Clint Eastwood, not Dirty Harry himself.

No, it was the same Mr. Eastwood who had lived in Carmel for over fourteen years.

I asked, "Well, why is he running? He is such a busy actor making all those movies, what is his agenda?"

She said, "He owns the Hog's Breath Inn and last year we rejected a development for a construction plan for a commercial building adjacent to his restaurant."

Finally, I started to see a glimmer of hope of some evidence, of using real information in a campaign of painting Clint Eastwood as having some alternative reason besides the well-being of the voters of Carmel.

Then much to my surprise, she said, "Oh no, we cannot go negative on Clint Eastwood. I want to run on my record. I think I can beat him on all the positive things that I have done for our City."

Well, you can imagine my thoughts running through my head. But I was impressed with this woman's bravery and spunk. She was going for it.

Later I found out Eastwood did everything right. His strategy was basic: he never attacked Mayor Townsend; he gave no national interviews; he stayed tightly involved in the community; and he did no paid advertising—just some buttons and bumper stickers. It was one of the most tasteful campaigns at that time. His slogan was simple "Bringing the Community Together."

His strategy worked. On April 8, 1986, with twice the voter turnout, Clint got a whopping 72.5 percent of the vote.

My only regret: that I never got to meet Dirty Harry in person.

Making a Contribution

Gerry Tyson

In 1976, I was dispatched by the Mo Udall presidential campaign to Springfield, Massachusetts to help the young coordinator there.

The campaign headquarters in a huge abandoned Five-n-Dime store. When I arrived, I noticed a large number of volunteers placing stamps on a mail piece.

I asked the coordinator where the main post office was located and asked him to take me there. I introduced him to Bulk Rate Permit.

I left the next day believing I had contributed to the campaign.

Who are My Friends?
Garry South

The word "friend" to politicians often has a very different meaning than it does to the average person. Most of us have heard the protocol-laden orations in the U.S. Senate where one Senator, who reputedly hates another one, nonetheless refers to him as "My friend, the Senator from the great state of Podunk—and he is my good friend, and despite our disagreements on policy, we always have been and always will be good friends, make no mistake about that."

Um, methinks the Senator doth protest too much?

It is also a sad fact of life in politics that many elected officials—perhaps because of their obsessive focus on their own career, a natural suspicion of other people and their motives, inadequate time and effort spent nourishing relationships—are essentially without true friends (Donald Trump comes to mind).

In 1998, I was managing Gray Davis's successful campaign for governor of California. In the primary that June, we had blown away two Democratic opponents and we even outpolled the one major Republican running.

Although Davis had been a fixture in California politics for twenty-five years—chief of staff to Governor Jerry Brown, two-term member of the State Assembly, two-term state controller, now the sitting lieutenant governor—he was still largely a mystery to most voters. Other than a couple of background factors of which he was especially proud, Davis was not one to talk candidly about himself or reveal his inner thoughts.

After our big primary victory, veteran *Los Angeles Times* political reporter Cathleen Decker, who had covered Davis's run for lieutenant governor four years earlier, asked to interview him about his personal life, kind of a "Who is the real Gray Davis?" inquiry.

I set up the interview in the conference room of our campaign headquarters in Los Angeles and joined Davis and Decker for the interview. At one point the questioning went like this:

DECKER: "So, Lieutenant Governor, who are some of the close personal friends you chum around with, that you could call up at the spur of the moment go to the Hollywood Bowl or a Dodgers game with?"

DAVIS: "You mean who are some my big supporters?"

DECKER: "No, no, I don't mean donors or campaign supporters or other elected officials, I mean just personal, non-political friends that you hang with in your down time."

DAVIS (putting his chin on his clasped fingers and looking at the ceiling): "Hmm, my close friends. Ummm, let's see."

Then, after what seemed like an awkward eternity, looking down the table to me he asked meekly: "Garry, who are some of my close personal friends that I hang with?"

Point made!

Decker, who is now campaign editor at the *Washington Post*, still brings this statement up and laughs about it to this day when we chat or have lunch.

Surprise!
Celinda Lake

In 2018, my firm was hired by Justice Democrats, a progressive political action committee, to do independent expenditures on behalf of Alexandria Ocasio Cortez's (AOC) primary campaign for the Democratic nomination for the House of Representatives.

We were hired to test her viability—could she win the primary against an incumbent? When we went to the district in Queens and the Bronx, every single store had a sign for her. It was just solid support for her, lining up with the diversity of the district. There was real momentum for her.

But we still thought, in the end, incumbents still win. In this case, the incumbent was Congressman Joe Crowley, who had served for two decades and was Chair of the House Democratic Caucus.

So, I was surprised when she won in a landslide, the biggest upset of the 2018 congressional election.

In retrospect, there were good reasons why it happened. Many voters in the district believed Crowley was going to run for Speaker of the House of Representatives, and many women thought he was going to challenge Speaker Nancy Pelosi for the job. That was a big negative. Meanwhile, Crowley had alienated the Bronx part of the district because he lived in Queens and didn't seem to care about them. He never campaigned in the Bronx and never come to see them. On Election Day, voters of color and Hispanics turned out in record numbers—especially in the Bronx.

Hotel Roosevelt
Jack Corrigan

During the 1988 Mike Dukakis presidential campaign, I thought our travel office was very inefficient and not always strategic about geographical choices. I always felt they spent more money than they should. It was wasteful.

I was stopping in Chicago on the way back from a trip to California when I finally put my foot down. I told the travel office, "I don't care where you put me, but if you put me at a hotel on Michigan Avenue, I'm going to make sure you get fired."

So, the travel office put me at the Roosevelt Hotel, which was somewhere on the South Side of Chicago, maybe fifteen blocks from downtown. I arrived at about two a.m. I had to walk past four pimps in the lobby. The bed had rubber sheets. I was only there for four hours, so it was Ok—but it actually wasn't Ok at all.

That was the last time that I tried to micromanage travel options.

Bill Randle, Mr. Scandal
David Heller

In 1998, Congresswoman Corrine Brown was running for re-election in Jacksonville, Florida. Her opponent was Bill Randle, a minister of a big church who had never run for office before. He started attacking Brown for poor attendance in Congress and missing votes. The Republicans put out a poll that had Randle up two percentage points in the district.

I said to the congresswoman, "I know we've never gone negative before, but we have to, we need to hit this guy."

She said, "You do what you got to do, I don't have any problem with it."

First of all, what does Randle rhythm with? "Scandal." So, the TV ad was "Bill Randle, he's Mr. Scandal."

We talked about a tax lien against his house and unpaid federal taxes. Then the kicker: Reverend Randle had a kid out of wedlock and had not paid child support.

I tracked down the kid and brought a film crew with me. We went up to the kid and put a microphone in his hand in front of his face, and asked, "Your daddy's going to see this, is there anything you want to say to him?"

The kid said, "I'd really like to see you some time."

We put that message on TV and we won the race fifty-nine to forty-one percent.

The Big Three

Jerry Austin

In the mid-1990s, I got a phone call from a friend of mine in California who had a piece of business for me. It wasn't political, which was pretty unusual, but it was welcomed. The client was the big three automakers in Detroit.

The governor of California, Pete Wilson, had issued an executive order requiring fifteen percent of all cars in California to be zero emission or electric cars by 2000. The big three automakers were all working on electric cars, but they didn't want a specific date by which their electric cars would be on the market.

They wanted me to come up with a plan to either have the governor rescind that executive order or extend the deadline. I drove to Detroit from Columbus, Ohio, where I was living, to meet with representatives of the big three companies. I had an idea.

I was into what I would call the "dead celebs" stage of my career. I used people who were dead as spokespersons for different candidates' causes: Albert Einstein, Edward R. Murrow, Thomas Jefferson, George Washington, and so forth.

My idea for the automakers was that the spokesperson would be Benjamin Franklin. Franklin, you know, discovered electricity, but this really wasn't brought to the forefront until Thomas Edison invented the light bulb two hundred years later.

Two out of the three automakers liked the idea, but the third one did not. They told me to come back on Monday with a better idea. It was Friday, so I went back to Columbus. I was really upset because that was my "A" material and I wasn't usually used to getting turned down with my "A" material. I spent the whole weekend trying to come up with some other idea, but I couldn't think of any.

So, I decided instead of driving to Detroit, I would fly to Detroit because I was very successful in coming up with ideas for TV spots on planes. But, instead of flying directly from Columbus to Detroit, I flew to Chicago and Chicago to Detroit, seeking more time. I got to Chicago, I had nothing. But by the time I landed in Detroit, I had it.

My idea was to create a radio spot that was a game show and it was called "Name the Inventor." The way that it was played is that I would name the invention, you'd tell me the inventor. I asked the executives to play along.

I said, "Who invented the automobile?"

Everybody said almost in unison, "Henry Ford."

I said, "Wrong."

"What do you mean wrong?"

"Henry Ford didn't invent the automobile. He invented mass production of the automobile. The automobile was invented in the 1880s by someone in Germany."

The Chrysler person said, "You know that for sure?"

I said, "No, I don't know that for sure, but I think that's what happened."

In those days, there was no Internet, so they sent out an intern. I don't know where the intern went, but he came back forty-five minutes later with the answer.

The intern said, "He's right. In 1884, German Yohan Price invented the automobile."

They approved my idea and recorded the radio ad.

Then they called and said, "You need to find out what radio station the governor listens to because we want to make sure he hears this ad."

I called some friends in California and found out the governor listened to National Public Radio. We obviously couldn't buy an ad on public radio. Instead, we bought other radio stations.

Governor Wilson rescinded the order.

III. Beginnings and Endings

I Got Here as Fast as I Could

Tom Vilsack

One day, Iliff King, the father of the late mayor of our city, Edward King, walked into my law office. Mr. King suggested I should run for mayor. He had deep concerns about the interim mayor appointed by city council, who he felt was not going to carry out his son's vision for the city. Also, he had watched me become involved with the community, and was impressed, even though I wasn't involved in politics.

I was not born or raised in Mt. Pleasant, Iowa. I had moved with my wife to her hometown of about eight thousand people in 1975. I soon found that I didn't have a name—I was the extension of somebody else. My wife had been the Homecoming Queen her senior year, so I was "Christine's husband." I was practicing law with her dad, so I was "Tom Bell's son-in-law." Always something other than Tom Vilsack.

So, I figured I needed to do something to establish my own name in the community. I was very interested in sports and our facilities for kids at the time were really subpar—actually dangerous. The showers were producing scalding hot water and had serious mold issues. The whole football field was unwalkable. Bond issues to fix these problems had repeatedly failed.

That's why I came home to my wife and told her: "Honey, I am going to raise the money myself to fix this problem."

She said there are three rules of success in Mt. Pleasant: first you need to have been born here; second you need to be Methodist; and third you need to be a Republican.

I was 0 for 3.

"Good luck," she said.

It was a magical time. I was just twenty-six years old. I got young people involved. I was a very firm believer in people having the passion to do the impossible because they don't know what they don't know.

We decided we needed $100,000. We took over the local radio station and kept the station all night instead of taking it off at midnight. I stayed up the entire weekend. By the time it was over, we had raised more than $206,000, almost entirely from individuals in the community.

All of the sudden this pipe dream took off. Labor unions committed to work for free. They had one requirement: "If you give us each a six-pack of beer, we can come after work and in the summer to help build this."

Then corporations saw that they needed to get involved with the project too. In the end, we had a $700,000 facility housing a track, a football field with beautiful turf, a baseball diamond, a softball field, and a place for the band to practice.

I did not become a Methodist or Republican. But I was elected mayor of Mount Pleasant in 1987.

When I ran for governor of Iowa in 1998, I had a sweatshirt that said, "I wasn't born here, but I got here as fast as I could."

Best Decisions
Curt Steiner

After I graduated from Ohio University, I decided I wanted to work for a Republican governor and to be the governor's spokesperson. It took me awhile to realize to get that job you have to help *elect* a governor. These opportunities only come around, like the Olympics, every four to eight years. So, it is about taking advantage of an opportunity which doesn't happen very often.

Eventually I found myself happily working eighteen hours every day for nearly two years on George Voinovich's 1990 Ohio gubernatorial campaign. Early in 1989, my friend Mike Dawson asked me, "Why are you so committed to this thing?"

I replied, "If we don't win this time, I may never be on a team that wins in my whole life, because it will be eight more years and I won't have the opportunity."

That spring I went to the Cleveland Indians home opener with Jerry Austin and Tom Fries. I knew I was going to work for George Voinovich, but Austin didn't know about it. We were talking about the gubernatorial election on the way to the game. I'll never forget Austin's comment: "We Democrats have the candidates, we have all the money, therefore Republicans win." I knew it was typical Austin reverse obvious.

Although George Voinovich was a popular mayor of Cleveland, he had experienced a humiliating defeat in 1988 when he ran a poor campaign for the U.S. Senate against Howard Metzenbaum. The people in Cleveland knew he was a good mayor, but in the rest of the state people thought he was just the guy that ran a really bad campaign. So, we had to improve Voinovich's image outside of the Cleveland area and re-introduce him to the other Ohio voters.

We needed to hire a media consultant and we ended up choosing Roger Ailes. Ailes was from Warren, Ohio and went to Ohio University—but we didn't hire him for those reasons. We decided to hire him because we thought he'd create the best possible ads for the Voinovich gubernatorial campaign. Back then, a lot of people hadn't met Roger Ailes and many that had didn't like him. But he was a fascinating guy to work with: he was a brilliant communicator and had the quickest wit of anybody I've ever met.

Roger made great negative ads for us, but the ads that mattered most were his positive ads. One such ad was called "Best Decision," a sixty-second ad created to convey that the "Best Decision" Voinovich ever made was marrying his wife Janet. Communicating that they had a good marriage was important for voters to know and helped improve Voinovich's image.

"Best Decision" was among the reasons Voinovich was elected governor in 1990—and I got the job I wanted.

How I Got Started in Politics
Rick Silver

I got interested in politics at a very early age, during the 1960 Kennedy-Nixon presidential race. I was eight years old and my family was on a cross-country trip to the west. We were in Las Vegas on Election Night. I was in the hotel room alone by myself and my parents were at a show or something. I could not take my eyes off the TV coverage and the closeness of the contest. The excitement, energy, and mystique of that night addicted me for the rest of my life.

In 1966, U.S. Senator Strom Thurmond ran for re-election as a Republican, having switched parties in 1964. I volunteered for his Democratic opponent, Bradley Morrah. I got to meet some important people, including Lt. Governor John West. West was a real gentleman, a real serious guy, a very conservative Democrat—a more personal conservative, you know, old school blue blood South Carolina type of thing—but also a player in Columbia.

In 1970, West appointed me as one of three high school seniors to serve as a floor page in the State Senate. I spent about two hours a day in high school, eight to ten a.m., and for the rest of the day, I worked in the Senate. It gave me an opportunity to have regular interactions with many of the senators. One, in particular was Earle Morris, who was a leading candidate for lieutenant governor when John West went for governor in 1970.

The floor page job paid fourteen dollars an hour and that was money to live on and operate when I went to college in 1970. Frankly, I eventually got my degree, but my education was oppressing. Instead, I enjoyed working out in the field, doing political things.

For both of these reasons, I wanted a paid job as a senior staffer for the 1970 campaign. Without talking to Senator Morris, I went to the campaign headquarters where Don Fowler was the campaign manager (and later chairman of the South Carolina Democratic Party and the Democratic National Committee).

I went up to Don and said, "I'm Earle's new boy, he wants you to bring me on." Don said, "Ok."

I quickly went back to the Senate that same afternoon to tell Earle that "Don just hired me, I'm his new boy, and I've been hired for your campaign."

Then I waited a couple few days of bated breath—they didn't talk to each other about it. It was only twenty years later at a reunion that I shared the truth with both of them, and they enjoyed it. That is how I got started in a serious capacity as a paid staffer.

In the 1970 campaigns for governor and lieutenant governor, West and Morris were separately nominated and elected for these posts.

It was a volatile, contentious, and sometimes violent year in South Carolina as it was in many parts of the country, and particularly in the South. It was a very close and hairy race. All of a sudden, after more than one hundred years of an all-Democratic state, there's a real threat of Republicans getting the governorship. It was a racially tinged race with desegregating the schools and busing as major issues and a Republican nominee just short of a self-avowed racist. The stakes were incredibly high.

Well, times were different then as a naive college freshman was about to find out. Notwithstanding the stakes, Earle was having an affair with dalliances being scheduled, all totally unbeknownst to moi. And this led to Earle's wife coming to

Columbia one evening and catching Earle with another woman in the act. And then I lost my "naivety." I will never forget being in the room when the situation was discussed, how to manage the issue, who could get to the wife, what to do if it came out, and how to develop a strategy with all of the conceivable contingencies.

Ultimately, with the last card in the deck, West's wife had to personally sit down with Earle's wife to ask, to beg, to cajole, to reason, to rationalize, "please don't make this a public issue, don't do anything." West's wife *did* make the difference. But West's wife never ever forgave Earle. It was a strange situation for a young person coming in to politics.

West was elected governor and was a good governor. Earl was elected lieutenant governor and was a decent lieutenant governor as well.

Oh, the end of the rest of the story is that Earle ended up getting a divorce and marrying the "other" woman.

Innovation and Revenge

Rick Silver

In 1974, I was working with my mentors on gubernatorial campaign of Lt. Governor Earle Morris. Don Fowler had resigned as chairman of the state Democratic Party to manage the campaign. The Democratic primary was supposed to be between Morris and a long-serving Congressman William Jennings Bryan Dolan, who was the epitome of a Southern politician of that time.

Enter Charles "Pug" Ravenel: a young fellow born in Charleston, South Carolina, but who had not lived in the state for twenty years. He was an investment banker and quite successful on Wall Street. He decided to come home to South Carolina and run for governor. Frankly, he was probably one of the first examples of someone who made his mark somewhere else, outside of politics, and then decided to make a difference by getting into politics—sort of Trump before Trump.

Ravenel teamed up with Marvin Chernoff. Marvin had been born in New York, grew up in Ohio, where he got involved in politics. He worked for Carl Stokes, the first African American mayor of Cleveland. Marvin went from being a businessman to getting a taste for politics to getting addicted to it. He and Pug had a mutual friend, who told Pug about Marvin—a guy who didn't have a twenty-year political résumé in campaigns and didn't do politics the conventional way. Pug and Marvin hit it off. Out of nowhere, Marvin packed his bags and came to South Carolina to run the Ravenel campaign for governor, starting with the Democratic primary.

Marvin did some very interesting things that had never been done before in South Carolina. Historically, it was a "political experience" state, for lack of a better term. It was the way you ran for office to go from courthouse to courthouse in all the forty-eight counties. The local office holders had great influence and particularly with it being a one-party Democratic state.

Marvin and Pug innovated in South Carolina. They ran a television campaign. Never happened before in South Carolina. They had bumper stickers everywhere. They got young people excited. It was largely a positive campaign, sort of hope and change for the state.

Of course, I was working with the old crowd. Everybody was convinced that it was a waste of money, that nobody's going to vote for you if they have not seen you in the right kind of places. I'll quote Don Fowler: "Rick, don't worry about those bumper stickers, they don't vote."

But Ravenel jumped ahead in the polls. We were watching his numbers double. It would go from two to four percent, four to eight percent, eight to sixteen percent— and it just kept doubling every time you would look at it. I didn't understand polls like I do now, looking at those kinds of numbers, and understanding what they meant.

At that time in South Carolina, like most Southern states, you had to get a majority to win the primary. If nobody got a majority, then there would be a runoff two weeks later between the top two candidates.

On Election Day, Ravenel finished first with about one-third of the vote, just slightly ahead of Bryan Dorn, who was second, with Earle Morris in third place. Pug then won the runoff by a solid majority. He never set foot in twenty-three of the forty-eight counties; he had never held a rally or did a parade in any of those counties. Instead, he and Marvin brought mass media into South Carolina politics.

The good old boys got their revenge. They found a clause in the state constitution that you had to be a resident and a citizen of South Carolina for five years before you could run or hold office. Ravenel had both voted and paid taxes while he lived in New York, and he had only come home a year before making his run. The South Carolina Supreme Court ruled against him and removed him from the ballot.

The Democrats had to hold a special convention to fill the ticket and Dorn was made the nominee. There was a bad public reaction to Ravenel being taken off the ticket; many voters felt that had been cheated.

Meanwhile, James Edwards, an unknown state senator from Charleston and one of the few Republican members of the State Senate, became the Republican nominee for governor by defeating retired General William Westmoreland in the GOP primary.

That set the stage!

It was a test of Republican strength, drawing on Strom Thurmond's switch to the Republican Party in 1964. The Democrats brought in Chernoff to help Dorn. But there was just too much resentment and it was too close to Election Day. Edwards won the general election: the first Republican governor elected in South Carolina in a hundred years.

When I Caught the Bug

Warren Tompkins

In the late 1960s, when I was still in college, my father and his law partner got involved in a local magistrate race where we lived in South Carolina. They dragged me into it. Back then magistrates ran in what were called "preferential primaries." It was technically non-binding, but magistrate candidates would run, and generally speaking, whoever won the primary would be nominated by the state senator from the area. Once a person was nominated, the governor would sign off on the nomination and make the appointment.

It was an eye-opening experience for me. It was vintage old-style Southern politics. It was day in and day out, paying people to go get them to vote. The other side was doing all this kind of stuff, too. Up to that point, just about everybody involved had been a Democrat, so the Democratic primary was the critical. But that was about to change. In 1974, there were contested primaries for the Republican and Democratic gubernatorial races.

State GOP leaders allied with U.S. Senator Strom Thurmond had been recruiting William Westmoreland to run for governor. He had been the U.S. Army chief of staff during the Vietnam War, and when he retired, he came home to Charleston, South Carolina. He was a horrible candidate. The first press conference when he announced his candidacy, someone asked him what he was going to do about education. He said, "Well, you have to ask to the party leaders about that." A typical general, he was a good delegator. He was just there to be out front. Somebody else was going to take care of all the issues. His campaign never recovered.

Meanwhile, GOP leaders not allied with Thurmond recruited their own candidate so Westmoreland wouldn't get the nomination by default. He was State Senator Jim Edwards, also from Charleston. He was in his first term in the State Senate and not very popular with the handful of Republicans then in the state legislature. Edwards was a dentist and had served in the Merchant Marine in World War II and later in the Naval Reserve.

The campaign was intense, but fewer than forty thousand people voted in the Republican primary—compared to several hundred thousand in the Democratic primary. There weren't a lot of Republicans in the state at that time.

Lo and behold, Edwards won the gubernatorial nomination by a big margin, with almost sixty percent of the vote. That's when we first came up with the name "The Charleston Crazies." I think Westmoreland won about every county in the state except Charleston. He got beat by a large margin in the Charleston County—the home turf of both candidates.

Edwards' win was a major upset, but not the only one that year. Over on the Democratic side, Charles "Pug" Ravenel finished first ahead of several better-known candidates and then won the runoff election. He was also from Charleston and had come back home from a successful finance career in New York to run for governor. But shortly before the general election, Ravenel was ruled off the ballot by the State Supreme Court because he hadn't resided in the state long enough to be an elected official. A special Democratic state convention nominated the second-place candidate, Congressman William Jennings Bryan Dorn.

Lo and behold, Edwards also wins the general election, with just about fifty percent of the vote. Nobody knew he was a Republican—in fact nobody knew much about him. Both candidates were conservative on the issues, but Dorn was the old establishment and Edwards was something new. There was a lot of discontent among voters. We had never had a Republican governor since Reconstruction.

Along with all this state-level turmoil, we had a very bitter race in our little community. The incumbent magistrate was a crook and trying to keep his job. People's cars were vandalized and lives were threatened. You couldn't keep a sign up because one side or the other was tearing it down. Just like the state level, one group was trying to maintain the old system and another group was trying to change it.

On Election Day, I was assigned as a poll watcher for our side. We used to have these great big voting machines. You could look at the back of the machine to tell you how many people had voted. It was one of those old-timey things. Somebody who obviously had a lot of experience told me, "Make sure when you go in the morning, get there before the polls open at seven a.m. Get there by six thirty if you can, at least by a quarter till seven. Then wander around and make sure you get a look at the back of all the machines to see if all of them are on zero."

I get in there that morning and I kind of wander around, introducing myself to everybody. I was the only person from my side there. The incumbent magistrate's secretary's husband was in the highway patrol, and he was lurking around in his uniform and fully loaded pistol. I went to look at the back of the machines and there was one where twenty-five people had already voted before seven o'clock.

I went over to the poll manager and said, "I'm not sure, something is not right." He said, "What do you mean?"

I said, "The machine over there has got votes on it and the polls aren't open yet. We can't use that machine unless we clear it—something has got to be done to clear that machine."

Oh my God, you would have thought that I dropped an atomic bomb in that place! Next thing I know, there were people coming from everywhere, all because of that dang machine. This was before cell phones, so I had a pocket full of quarters in case I had to use the pay telephone. I called my father's office. My father and his partner came over at about ten o'clock.

Daddy asked me, "Are you alright?"

I said, "Yeah, why?"

"We just got a call," my father said, "telling us that if we knew what was good for us, we would get you out of the polling place. Something bad might happen to you."

I said, "Hey, don't worry about me. I hadn't seen anyone walk through here I can't handle." I had a baseball bat and a shotgun in the trunk of my car out in the parking lot. If I could get to the parking lot, I was going to be all right. We won the race, of course.

Because I knew many of the young, up and coming Republican operatives, I was able to connect with Governor Edwards about our magistrate candidate. I said, "Hey, this guy is good, how about signing off on that magistrate appointment?" I laid out the story about what all we had gone through. Edwards appointed our guy.

That's when I caught the bug. You do the mechanics of a campaign, then it's election night, the thrill of victory, and all that stuff.

I said to myself, "Man, I need to find a way to do this all the time!"

Job Interview
Jack Walsh

During Jimmy Carter's 1980 re-election campaign, I came home from work and my son Christopher, age nine, says, "Daddy, Daddy, the mayor called, the mayor called."

I said, "Well, what does he want?"

"He wants you to call him!"

Kevin White was then the mayor of Boston, Massachusetts. So, I call White and I said, "Did you call me?"

He said, "No, I didn't call you."

I hang up the phone and say to my son, "Christopher, how did you know it was the mayor?"

And he said, "Oh, he was a really nice guy, he told me a story about bunnies."

I say to myself and my wife, "Kevin White never told a kid a story about bunnies in his life. He doesn't do bunny stories."

I asked Christopher, "How do you know it was the mayor?"

"He called from his house!"

"What do you mean from his house?"

"It was a call from White's house."

"Oh, it's from the White House."

So, I called the general number at the White House, and say, "This is Jack Walsh returning a phone call."

Soon President Carter comes on the line and says, "Thanks for calling back. Our campaign needs you to talk to Hamilton Jordan."

I say, "Do you mind if I ask you a question?"

"Not at all," the president said.

"Where did you get my name and number?"

"Tip O'Neill gave it to us. Tip O'Neill said you're the best."

"No kidding. Why did you think he did that?"

"Well, Tip said our campaign needs some help on communicating with real Democratic people."

Then Carter asked, "What do you think the problem is?"

"Well, you know I'm not working for you, but I voted for you," I said. "I think the problem is you. I think you need to learn how to connect to the Democratic base. I don't think you really know how to get to the Black community. I don't think you really know how to talk to working-class Democrats, like union people in the Midwest."

I wasn't trying to insult him—just telling him the truth from my perspective.

After the call ends, my phone rings within a minute.

It's Tip O'Neill.

"Who the f*** do you think you are?"

"What are you talking about Tip?"

"Do you know you were talking to the president of the United States and you were giving him instructions on how to run a campaign and how to be a Democrat?"

"What did you want me to do, kiss his ass?"

Within a week, I was hired on the national campaign staff.

Serendipity
Dale Butland

My route to national politics was, to say the least, serendipitous.

I earned a bachelor's degree in psychology at a little school in Texas called Abilene Christian. The month I graduated—May of 1970—the Kent State shootings happened. And that event was the first thing that changed my life's trajectory. Prior to Kent State, I had planned to go to graduate school in clinical psychology, but the shootings upset me so deeply that I decided to go to graduate school in political science instead.

I got my master's degree in international relations from George Washington University in Washington D.C. and finished everything but my dissertation for my Ph.D. from the University of Chicago. At that point, I got a job offer at the Chicago Council on Foreign Relations to run a new program for some of the many Fortune 500 companies headquartered in that city. My job was to arrange for speakers to come to the city from Washington D.C. and abroad who would speak on topics that were relevant and timely for these large businesses. They could be officials from the treasury, commerce, or state departments, for example, as well as ambassadors, other diplomats and folks in non-government organizations from around the world. Corporations would pay an annual fee to be a part of this program and, in return, their executives would get up-to-the-minute information important to them.

As it turned out, this experience would change my life as well.

One of the people I brought to Chicago was Stanley Marcus, the Assistant Secretary of Commerce for International Trade. As it happened, Stan and I had a mutual friend in Chicago—with whom Stan had worked in the U.S. Senate, prior to his joining the Carter administration. So, while Stan was in town, this mutual friend invited the two of us for a dinner at his home.

Marcus and I hit it off so well at dinner that night that by the time the evening ended, he asked if I'd like to come to Washington D.C. and be his Special Assistant at the Commerce Department. So off to Washington D.C. I went, joining the Carter administration as a political appointee in the Department of Commerce. That was December of 1978. I stayed for a little over a year—until it became increasingly clear that Carter would not be re-elected in the 1980 election.

I started looking around for my next gig, figuring that Capitol Hill might be a good place to start. Along with a horde of other job-seekers, I walked the halls of Congress, dropping my résumé off with pretty much every Democratic officeholder who would take it. I've often said that getting your foot in the door in Congress is pretty much a matter of timing and luck. It's walking into an office where they happen to need someone with your skill set. And if you can somehow wrangle an interview—and impress them—they would just hire you, instead of combing through all the stacks of résumés they had collected.

Since my parents had moved to Ohio in 1970, I was making the rounds with the Ohio congressional delegation. I interviewed with then-Congressman Don Pease (who was on the House Foreign Affairs Committee) and a bunch of others—but was getting nowhere. Meanwhile, my mother was dating a fellow named Joe Sedivy (my dad had passed away in 1974), who was Secretary Treasurer of the Ohio Building Trades union. Joe was able to get me an interview with John Glenn's office or, more specifically, with Glenn's chief of staff, Bill White.

At the interview, I tried to pass myself off as a legislative assistant in the area of international affairs (Senator Glenn served on both the Senate Foreign Relations and the Senate Intelligence Committees). After ten minutes or so, I could see Bill's eyes kind of glazing over—and I realized that he was only giving me a courtesy interview as a favor to Joe Sedivy. So right at the end of my interview, I threw a Hail Mary pass and mentioned that I thought I "wrote a pretty good speech, too."

At that, Bill perked up a bit and said, "Really, who have you written for?"

And I said, "Well, I wrote for my boss at the Commerce Department, and I also wrote a bit for the Secretary of Commerce, Juanita Krebs." White asked if I had any samples of my writing—which I immediately sent to him. I didn't know at the time that Glenn happened to be looking for a speechwriter.

After reviewing my material, Bill White called me back for a second interview at which time he also introduced me to the Senator. The interview went well, and a couple of days later I was offered a job as Glenn's speechwriter with a secondary portfolio as Legislative Assistant for Small Business—something I knew absolutely nothing about.

In May of 1980, I began working on Capitol Hill, writing speeches for a genuine national hero and one of the most famous U.S. Senators in the country.

I now look back at some of my early speechwriting efforts—and they're just short of awful. Ponderous, boring, and far too academic in tone. But I got better as time went on, and Glenn, who had a reputation as a boring and bland public speaker, started to get better reviews from the news media. Still, he was John Glenn and he remained a pretty wooden speaker. In fact, I always said that being John Glenn's speechwriter was kind of like being boxing promoter Don King's barber: you don't want to tell anyone.

After his overwhelming re-election to the Senate in 1980, John decided to run for president in 1984. I was the campaign's chief speechwriter and hired a small team of assistants to keep up with the crushing workload of a presidential effort.

Obviously, the campaign didn't go as well as we hoped—and John was forced to drop out of the race in the spring of 1984 without a single primary win to our credit.

At that point, of course, all of the "hired guns" who had been running our campaign began to head for the exits—including a fellow named Greg Schneider who had served as Glenn's campaign press secretary.

Returning to his Senate duties, Glenn clearly needed a press secretary. So, I went to John and said, "I think I can do that job—I think I can be your press secretary."

Glenn said, "Really, you think you can do that?"

I said, "Yeah, I do."

He said "Well, I'll tell you what—let's try it for six months and see if it works out."

And that's how I became John Glenn's press secretary in the summer of 1984, a job I held until January 1999, when John retired from the Senate.

Getting Started in Politics

Sarah Kovner

After college, I moved to New York City. I needed to get involved in New York politics. I looked in the yellow pages of the telephone book—and people don't even know what the yellow pages are now. I looked under political organizations. I found one near my home, but they never answered the phone. I looked for one nearby where I was working. I found the Lexington Democratic Club, which was the wealthiest Democratic club in the city. They had a staff person. It was in what was called the "silk-stocking district," where John Lindsay was the Congressman (he was eventually a Republican mayor of New York City).

I got involved immediately. I ran the campaign for the candidate for State Assembly. Of course, she didn't win: it was a very Republican district.

After a few months, I said, "Well, I'm going to go down to Greenwich Village and work to beat Carmine DeSapio." He was the most powerful political boss in New York State, the leader of Tammany Hall. His power rested on an inverted pyramid from Greenwich Village, which is where he was a district leader, but then he was Manhattan County leader as well as Secretary of State, appointed by the Democratic governor, Averell Harriman. In addition, DeSapio was the national committeeman from New York, when there was one woman and one man from each state appointed to the Democratic National Committee. By one means or another, he controlled many government jobs.

I went to Greenwich Village and I presented myself to that club, the Village Independent Democrats. I was hired to be part of the campaign for district leader against DeSapio in 1959. We lost, but it was very close.

In 1960, I ran and was elected to the Democratic state committee as a representative from my assembly district. In New York State, we had state conventions to pick candidates to run for statewide office in the 1960s. I was a delegate.

Mayor Robert Wagner Jr. was an enormous force within the Democratic Party. He had a wonderful assistant named Marcy O'Rourke. O'Rourke was the head of the Board of Elections. On some lower nominations, he told various officials in the New York City delegation, "Mayor Wagner would like you to vote for X. Mayor Wagner would like you to vote for Y. Mayor Wagner would like you to vote for Z." He gets to me and said, "Sarah, Mayor Wagner would like you to vote for whomever you think best."

Wagner was a progressive. His father was the great U.S. Senator Robert Wagner. He tried to avoid controversy. His attitude was if you let something sit around enough, it usually goes away. He was very careful.

But in 1961, Wagner decided to oppose Carmine DeSapio. The district had a large Italian population and was the base of DeSapio's power. We decided to go right to the heart of the Italian district with Mayor Wagner on a walking tour. We were all very nervous. People started coming out of buildings and congratulating Wagner; people were waving at him from fire escapes. He got a great reception. He was the mayor. He was in their neighborhood walking the streets and greeting people.

We beat DeSapio. In retrospect, he was a good leader. We didn't appreciate what we had until he was gone.

My First Political Job

Mark Weaver

I was a graduate student working on a master's degree in political science. You'd think I'd know about politics, but I had never worked on a campaign before.

One night I was in my apartment and nothing good was on TV.

So, I call my mother, "Hey Mom, what's new? How are you?"

She said, "This fellow, Jon Fox, wants to run for office and he seems really nice. He's running for state representative in our hometown. I think you'd really like him. You should probably volunteer on a campaign."

I said goodbye and got to thinking about her suggestion. I typed up a two-page letter to Jon Fox. "I know the district because I grew up there," I wrote. "I'm getting my master's in political science. I'd like to work on your campaign. Here's the strategy for how you can win."

Two days later, Fox called me. The town was about two hours away. I drove to meet him in this beat-up 1970 VW Bug that had holes in the floor. I had no money, a credit card for gas, and a little change in the ashtray that I would use for tolls.

He met me at a country club. I'd never been to a country club before. I have on a sports coat and a button-down shirt, tie and khakis—no belt because I didn't know you were supposed to wear a belt with dress pants. Fox invites me to order lunch. I order a cheesesteak.

I start talking. Everything I'm saying he is writing down. He said what I said was the most brilliant thing he'd ever heard. I was shocked. He's taking detailed notes on small slips of paper and then shoving them into his pocket. I start to lose focus on the political talk because the bill was coming and I assumed I would have to at least pay for mine.

I was losing track and imagining I could run to the car and get some change and hope I have enough. I figured the cheesesteak would be about nine bucks. I didn't know you can't pay with cash at a country club and that he was going to pay. I had no idea at the time.

I was very distracted when he said, "That was great, you need to start working on the campaign immediately! On Saturday there's going to be a strategy meeting right here in this country club. Could you come up from graduate school at eight a.m.? It's really important!"

I said, "Why yes that's great!"

I had never worked on a political campaign and had nothing except what I learned in college and grad school and what I had seen on TV and read in books. I spent the rest of the week doing research and writing strategy. I imagined the introduction, "Attention ladies and gentlemen, we bring to you this graduate student who's a brilliant political strategist."

I got there early. Fox said, "Mark, I'm so glad you're here!"

We step inside. He says, "See those folding chairs? I need those in rows of ten. Here's fifteen dollars, go get some donuts for everyone."

What I then realized was that he needed me to set up chairs and buy donuts. Those notes he was taking was what he did to everyone so that it looked like he was listening carefully when he really wasn't.

I set up the chairs and bought the donuts.

I eventually made it into his inner circle. He then hired me full-time to do political strategy. He won three-to-one in a district with quite a few Democrats, and he went on to serve in Congress. Later he and I became very close friends.

Beres, Not Perez
Tom Beres

When I became the editor of the Westlake, Ohio high school newspaper, and was fortunate enough to earn financial assistance to matriculate at Northwestern University, I assumed I would have some sort of reporting career.

I had summer jobs at the Cleveland Press—the afternoon newspaper in Cleveland, Ohio. My title was copy boy. The major responsibility was to be the gofer for all the editors, columnists, and reporters. My first job was basically sharpening legendary columnist Dick Feagler's pencil and getting him coffee. There were seven editions every day. Every time an edition came out, I'd have to snatch that edition coming off the presses and deliver them to all the necessary personnel to review and evaluate.

There was a presumption that I would work for the Cleveland Press. But when I graduated from Northwestern, I had an opportunity to return for a fifth year and take primarily broadcasting courses. I had a great experience. I participated in a program at their Washington D.C. Bureau, feeding stories to WMAQ, the NBC radio station in Chicago. The assignment consisted of interviewing members of the Illinois congressional delegation and Senators Charles Percy and Adlai Stevenson regarding their thoughts about the day's developments and Watergate hearing revelations. I didn't realize at the time what a significant chapter of U.S. history was unfolding.

After receiving my degree, my objective was to secure a job in Ohio, and preferably the Cleveland television market. I forwarded résumés, audition tapes, and interview materials to all the TV news directors in Ohio.

The first response I received was from a new news director of a TV station in Dayton. He had just fired his entire reporting staff and was in the process building a new staff that was energetic, diverse, and cheap. The diversity factor came into play.

I drove to Dayton figuring I had next to no chance of getting the job but that the interview would be good experience. This was midsummer. I was working a nighttime radio news job and spent lots of my daytime off-hours hanging out at the apartment pool. So, I had a *very* dark suntan, which apparently got noticed.

The news director began the interview with "Well, Mr. Perez, we've looked at your credentials and they seem very impressive. Just a couple questions: Mr. Perez have you ever covered labor unions?"

"I've had some experience, and by the way, the correct pronunciation of my name is Beres."

"Mr. Perez, when you were a suburban reporter, did you cover local governments—you know, county governments?"

"I do have some experience; the correct pronunciation is Beres."

"Mr. Perez. . .."

After about four or five times of attempting to correct him about my name, I thought "Well, I'm not misrepresenting anything, yet he has obviously come to some erroneous conclusion that I was Hispanic."

About a week after being hired, I met with the personnel director.

He said, "You said you were Puerto Rican."

"No, I didn't," I replied.

When my new boss realized he'd hired a Caucasian Hungarian/Ukrainian instead of a Hispanic, he went ballistic.

So, my forty-seven-year checkered broadcast career covering mainly local, state and election year politics was launched by a case of mistaken ethnic identity.

I had the good fortune to be hired in what, in my mind at the time, is still a decent size city for a first TV job.

A Wakeup Moment

Steve Rosenthal

I started in my twenties with the Communication Workers of America (CWA) in New Jersey in 1981. We organized state, county, and local government workers. We had just organized thirty-eight thousand state workers, fifteen thousand county and local government workers, and represented a bunch of AT&T and Bell workers. All of a sudden, we were a very big union in a very small state.

Reverend Jesse Jackson was really close to Jan Pierce, assistant to the regional vice president of CWA. Pierce asked Jackson to appear at a rally on the Statehouse steps in Trenton, New Jersey. We were supposed to fly him to Trenton by helicopter from New York. But there was a really bad electrical storm and the helicopter couldn't fly. So, Jackson had to take the train to Trenton. Then something happened with Amtrak—the time didn't work or whatever. Then he was on a milk train to Trenton. You know how pleased he was, in August, to be on the New Jersey transit train making every stop on the way to Trenton with the air conditioning system out. It was a nasty train ride.

There are five thousand people in front of the Statehouse waiting for Jackson's arrival. We're delaying, delaying, delaying—trying to keep them occupied so they don't leave. Jackson was the main attraction.

At the same time, we were also working on an initiative campaign to change the city charter in New Brunswick, New Jersey. Johnson & Johnson was then headquartered there and they controlled the city. All of the council members are elected at-large, which was a way to keep African American citizens off the council. We had a campaign going to change the city charter to elect all the council members by wards. All the local ministers were getting a lot of money from Johnson & Johnson and weren't eager to support our initiative.

We had an idea: we'd get all the ministers to Trenton. We'd have them waiting in a hotel room. Jackson would meet with them and urge them to support the charter change.

Jackson finally arrived at the train station in Trenton. We ushered him to a waiting car. A friend of mine was driving; I was sitting in the passenger seat; Pierce and Jackson were in the back. I was supposed to brief Jackson about the ministers' meeting as we drove to the Statehouse. I looked at him and told him all about the charter campaign. He barely looked at me; he was basically sweating. When I'm done briefing him, he says "I was working on charter change elections before you were born." I just shut up the rest of the way there.

The crowd had dwindled a bit, but there were still a few thousand people left. Jackson, he knocks it out of the ballpark. We got to the hotel to meet with the ministers and Jackson literally knocked the thing out of the ballpark again. He laid it on the line for them, explaining why they needed to support the charter change campaign. It couldn't have been better.

It was a wakeup moment for me: I never underestimated Jesse Jackson again.

Queen Elizabeth and the Bottle of Cheap Gin
Sal Russo

After serving as the political consultant for the successful 1982 George Deuk-mejian for Governor campaign in California, I took a leave of absence from my firm to serve as the new governor's deputy chief of staff. Among other responsibilities, I handled dealing with the Reagan White House and any foreign governments.

Shortly after taking office, I brought my office bar setup into the governor's office and asked the governor whether he wanted it in his private study or in the larger adjoining Cabinet Room, now called the Ronald Reagan Cabinet Room. This is where Governor Reagan kept a bar during his tenure and where I sometimes served as bartender when working for Reagan.

The governor informed me that he didn't think we should have alcoholic beverages in the governor's office. I told him that it would be ridiculous to follow Jimmy Carter's example. He had banned alcohol from the White House. I asked him what are we going to do when legislators, lobbyists, and others come down after work and want a drink. He said he would offer coffee.

I decided that arguing any further would be fruitless, but I knew that he would relent as more and more people showed up at his office and expected an after-work cocktail, which was a common social habit during that period of time.

Simultaneously, I received a phone call from Mike Deaver, the Deputy Chief of Staff to President Reagan, my former supervisor during my tenure working for

Governor Reagan. Mike informed me that Queen Elizabeth and Prince Phillip would be visiting California on an official visit and that President and Mrs. Reagan wanted me to make sure that everything was handled properly without a faux pas. He sternly reminded me that this visit was important to the Reagans and they were counting on me.

One of the events planned for the Queen and Prince included a luncheon in the State Capitol Rotunda, a highly prized occasion that brought a phenomenal amount of demand for tickets. Prior to the luncheon, the Queen was given the governor's private office, rest room, and cabinet room for a break; Prince Phillip was given a nearby staff conference room to serve his needs.

Governor Deukmejian, Mike Deaver, and I retreated to my office, which had served as Deaver's office during Reagan's tenure as governor, where we waited in preparation for the upcoming grand entrance into the Rotunda with the Queen and Prince. Shortly thereafter, one of the Queen's attendants entered and whispered in Mike's ear. He turned to the governor and said, "Governor, Queen Elizabeth and Prince Phillip would each like a gin and tonic."

At this point, Governor Deukmejian was sitting on my credenza, which when opened revealed a fully equipped bar. Knowing of the governor's admonition of "no alcohol" in the governor's office, I quickly debated whether my higher calling was to the governor, who was my direct employer, or to the president, who had put me on special assignment.

Finally, I looked at the governor and said, "If you get off my credenza, I think I can solve this problem." The governor was clearly perplexed but climbed off. I opened it up and revealed the full bar.

When I looked in the credenza to determine whether we had gin, I noticed only a very cheap, inexpensive bottle that had been used in a punch for a summer party. It was "Gemco" brand, which was the name of a membership low-cost department store then in operation.

When I pointed it out to Mike, he said, "Pour it up. It's all you have." So that's what I did. We had to retrieve two cafeteria glasses and ice, use my finger as an effective stir stick, and handed the Queen's attendant two gin and tonics.

About fifteen minutes later, the Queen's attendant came back and whispered in Mike's ear. Mike turned to me and said, "They want the whole bottle."

I said to Mike, "we can't possibly give them the bottle, since they will see what a horrendous brand of gin we are serving them."

Mike said, "They won't know; they will think it is a premiere American brand that they never heard of; they would never think that we would be serving them inferior gin."

With that, I presented the Queen's attendant with the nearly full bottle of gin.

After the successful Capitol Rotunda luncheon was finished, the Queen was going on to tour Yosemite National Park. The rest of us retreated to the governor's office, which had served as a rest area for the Queen, and ultimately Prince Phillip, and where they enjoyed their "refreshments."

The first thing we noticed upon entering the adjoining Cabinet Room was a nearly depleted bottle of gin. We wondered if that much cheap gin could have been consumed by two people.

In any event, Mike turned to me and said, "I don't want to ever read about this until both Ron and Nancy are gone." And so, I honored my pledge that I would refrain from telling the story publicly until now, although I think that President Reagan would have a good laugh about it all—but probably not Nancy.

As a side note, the governor never mentioned to me my disobedience during his term in office, but it has been a source of a few good laughs at subsequent office reunions. The governor did finally relent a few months later about providing California wine during formal lunches in the Ronald Reagan Cabinet Room. I fulfilled his request without revealing that I already had most of the cupboards filled with wine donated by the Wine Institute before he had taken office.

The Agony of Defeat

William Sweeney

Election Day 1980 was the end of the most painful year in my professional experience to that point. The Democratic Party had engaged in a civil war between President Jimmy Carter and Senator Ted Kennedy. It wasn't just a political fight over the nomination and the scars would last a generation. The Democratic congressional majority in both chambers was challenged by the Republicans with a range of ideological, generational, and skilled candidates—many without any public experience or records.

The bottom fell out of the Democratic campaign at the Cleveland debate, when President Carter decided to share his discussions with his teenage daughter about the danger of nuclear arms control. Ronald Reagan's calming, mature presence as a credible alternative choice doomed the Carter re-election campaign and eventually many other Democrats down ballot.

By Monday night, field reports from congressional campaigns and a range of political consultants revealed consistent weakening and increasing worries about Election Day.

On Tuesday morning, I had two long phone calls. Speaker O'Neill and I reviewed the situation of all the major challenges to Democratic members of the House of Representatives. I was worried about Carter, but thought incumbents winning re-election was still a good bet, which was statistically true, except for 1974. The straight Republican vote of Reagan-Senate-House did not seem to be a tide that morning. It's a conversation I always regret. I wish I had been more pessimistic and perhaps more direct about the collapse of the Carter campaign.

John White, the Chairman of the Democratic National Committee, called to have a similar review. What was striking was that John clearly seemed to think Democrats were going to lose. He felt the links between the assorted Republican campaigns were underway and there was a possible major defeat at hand. What I didn't know then was that there was a major poll in selective circulation in the Carter Administration which forecast a major defeat.

Election Day afternoon was a combination of conversations around the country about the usual turnout indicators, where there were no meaningful available numbers, and then the leaks of the assorted network exit polls, which changed every few hours. There were some places where the conversations and exit polls seemed to reinforce each other. Indiana had the Bayh-Quayle Senate race and a number of close congressional races. I remember checking in with those campaigns and coming away convinced we were in for a long night.

Tuesday afternoon, I received a summons to come to the White House for a meeting in Hamilton Jordan's office. I was told that "the president is aware of the outcome and wants to get it over with as quickly as possible." The Democratic Election Night event was at the Sheraton and the president wanted to deliver his concession speech early.

The request was that I should alert the speaker and ask him to be prepared to join the president. Voting was still underway on the East Coast and I knew O'Neill's personal stories about declaring victory early affecting races on the West Coast. I told the group O'Neill would be adamant and would not join the president before polls closed in California. Hamilton told me the president was determined to put this speech behind him.

It was over.

I left the White House and walked to the basement of the Hay Adams Hotel, where I knew there were pay phone booths with doors. No cell phones in 1980! I also was concerned about being followed from the White House since I might go to the media—standard Washington D.C. practice. I called the speaker's office and told the staff that I had just left the White House and needed to see the speaker as soon as possible. I would come directly to his Capitol office. I had been Executive Director of the Democratic Congressional Campaign Committee (DCCC) since July 1977 and had only requested an immediate meeting with the speaker a few times. After checking with the speaker, she said to come to the office.

The cab ride to the Capitol seemed exceptionally long because I knew O'Neill and his staff were simply going to explode. Relations with the Carter White House were routinely awful and this request would simply confirm all their bad experiences and negative judgments about the Carter team's political expertise.

I told the speaker about the meeting and the president's request. O'Neill's response was volcanic, immediate, and negative. His past experiences with damaging turnout in the West with news from the East were repeated to me a few times.

I left the speaker and called Hamilton. I reported the speaker was absolutely determined to follow the election returns from his office in the Capitol and make no statements until polls closed in California. Hamilton asked, "If the president called, would it make a difference?" I advised him not to expose the president to such a conversation because the speaker's attitude was firm.

Polls started closing in Kentucky and Indiana at seven p.m. (EST) and the Reagan vote was stronger than the afternoon exit polls.

By seven thirty p.m. (EST), the networks were calling the election for Reagan and the congressional losses were trickling in from around the country.

The announcement that President Carter had left the White House to make a concession speech became a national news event.

Reports of defeats came from congressional campaigns and assorted Democratic state party leaders calling in to my DCCC office. The generational targeting by the Republicans had a clear impact and there were also a few surprise Republican candidates who borrowed money for late media. In a tidal-wave year (we didn't know about a "tsunami" in 1980), one party loses all the close races. That pattern was part of the night's story. A particularly sad story for me were all the defeated women congressional candidates, especially Lynn Cutler in Iowa.

As President Carter was preparing to concede, my phone lines jumped to life. On one line, I had Speaker O'Neill exploding about the Carter concession's impact on the party and the House; on the second line, Jim Corman was telling me he was certain the race was lost; and, on the third line Phil Burton—among the most intense people I ever knew—was screaming, swearing, and exceptionally angry about what was happening. After listening to "dogshit" more than a dozen times, I left Burton on hold to take O'Neill's call. When I reconnected with Phil a few minutes later, he was still screaming and hadn't noticed I had been off the call.

The hardest personal chapters of the evening were the reports from Jim Corman's campaign in the San Fernando Valley. Jim was the DCCC Chairman who took the risk to make this twenty-six-year-old the executive director. Jim had been a member of the Kerner Commission and was one of the members of Congress who went South marching for civil, economic, and voting rights. Early in his career he changed committee assignments to join the Judiciary Committee to help write the civil rights laws. Jim was in a fight over busing with Bobbi Fiedler, a local school board member.

I had been heavily involved in changing his campaign and staff from its "family" nature to a professional operation led by Clint Reilly, as well as raising over a million dollars for a House seat, which, in 1980, made the campaign among the most expensive congressional campaigns in the country. I was almost fired twice over the course of that campaign year because his older congressional staff resented my influence and impact on the campaign.

As the race closed in the last week, the campaign wanted to borrow several hundred thousand dollars to go on Los Angeles network television—there was no cable in 1980. I wouldn't put Jim's personal future at risk and turned down the proposition. When President Carter conceded the election, it was still afternoon in the San Fernando Valley, but people stopped waiting in line to vote because the election was "over." We had Democratic precincts where Jim received over eighty percent of the vote and then not one vote was cast in the final two hours. People simply drove home after work. Jim lost by about seven-hundred and fifty votes in a district with sixty-two percent Democratic registration, but racially divided by the politics of busing and desegregation.

The night had a few more hours of bad political news. Democrats lost control of the Senate, which was a surprise to all, and thirty-five seats in the House.

Walking home to my Capitol Hill apartment at midnight, I was trying to absorb the impact of the losses while anticipating the fury about to be released over the next day, weeks, and months.

In retrospect, a personal conclusion is that President Carter's unnerving comments about discussing nuclear weapons with his daughter in Cleveland, plus his selfish determination to "get it over with" on election night, cost the Democrats the Senate and several House seats in the West, including Jim Corman. Personal memoirs and political scientists have mixed conclusions, but that's my two cents.

Four years later, in the closing months of the 1984 Mondale campaign, I was assigned to the Democratic Victory Fund located at 2121 Wisconsin Avenue, NW, appropriately overlooking a graveyard.

For election night 1984, I was in St. Paul coordinating the events for the Mondale/Democratic Party major donors. The vice president visited our group about five p.m. and spent well over an hour with a collection of people who had made asking for dollars for Mondale part of their daily life for years. He knew the campaign was lost, but said he wouldn't make any remarks until polls closed in California. Mondale was a real national political party leader.

After Vice President Mondale left, we moved to a dining room with television sets so we could watch the returns while dining. NBC's Tom Brokaw came on and said the network would not make projections until all the polls had closed, a proposed reform since 1980.

But at 8:01 p.m. (EST), the entire electoral map east of the Mississippi turned "red" and Brokaw announced Reagan had won re-election—before results were reported from the Central Time Zone or any state west of the Mississippi.

IV. Politics

The Mummers Parade
Mark Siegel

One of the major issues that divided the regular wing and the reform wing of the Democratic Party during the period the Democrats were drafting their party charter was whether to mandate that the party hold a midterm policy conference before midterm elections. That concept was imbued in the European Party Government model. In European parties, such party issue conferences are held almost annually. The Democratic Charter adopted in 1974 skirted the issue by saying that the Democratic Party "may" hold such conferences in the period between national nominating conventions, but they were not mandated.

In 1982, the Democrats met in Philadelphia for the second (and probably the last) such conference in party history. The gathering was viewed as a testing ground for prospective 1984 presidential candidates to present their messages and strut their wings. As one of his most outspoken supporters on the Democratic National Committee (DNC), U.S. Senator Ted Kennedy asked me to organize his operation for Philadelphia.

On the day before the convention, representatives of presidential candidates met with DNC Chairman Chuck Manatt to agree on the terms of their respective candidates' participation. It was agreed that all candidates would have thirty minutes to address the conference. Each representative chose the time of the speech during the

Friday night through Sunday afternoon during the conference. And each candidate representative was given the opportunity to select the music that would be played by the orchestra as the candidate was introduced. I asked that Senator Kennedy make the closing speech on Sunday. As a traditionalist, I requested that the orchestra play *Happy Days Are Here Again*. (U.S. Senator Alan Cranston's staff selected *Chariots of Fire*, which I thought was both odd and funny.)

The conference proceeded without drama on Friday and Saturday, with the orchestra blasting the chosen music when the candidates made their thirty-minute addresses. Everyone waited with great anticipation for Sunday's closing program and the closing speech from the presumptive front-runner for the Democratic nomination, Ted Kennedy.

I arrived early on Sunday morning to check on logistics and set up our operation. I noticed that the orchestra pit was empty except for one man sitting there with an accordion. I went over and asked him where the orchestra was.

He said, "I am the orchestra."

I assumed there was some sort of an error and tracked down Chairman Manatt at the conference headquarters hotel. I said something like "Chuck, where is my orchestra?"

He smiled and said, "I didn't promise you an orchestra, I promised you music and that's what you're getting, music from the accordion."

I said, "Seriously?"

He just grinned in response. I was infuriated.

I went back to the Kennedy staff room and gathered our staff. I explained that Chairman Manatt had screwed us and we didn't have an orchestra. I told the staff that we were going to find an orchestra and get them into the conference. One staffer broke in and said the Philadelphia Mummer's band, famous for their music and their fez hats, were scheduled to play later that day in a nearby hotel. I immediately dispatched him to talk to the Mummers and ask them if they would do Ted Kennedy a little favor. An hour later he returned to report they were on board.

At the closing ceremony the conference hall was packed with delegates waiting for the Kennedy speech. Chairman Manatt gaveled the conference to order and introduced "the senior Senator from Massachusetts, Edward Moore Kennedy." The little accordion man in the orchestra pit began to play *Happy Days Are Here Again*, which could barely be heard in the massive room.

Suddenly, the center doors to the hall opened and forty members of the Mummers Band, dressed in full regalia with fez on their heads, marched into the Hall. Around their necks they wore the official credentials to the 1982 Democratic National Policy Conference of the members of Congress (that I had in my possession all along). The Mummers marched in playing a rousing rendition of *Happy Days Are Here Again*. The delegates went wild.

Chairman Manatt from the podium started banging his gavel screaming, "Who are those people? Get them out of here!"

But the Mummers were there to stay marching up and down the aisles of the convention in between cheering and singing delegates as Ted Kennedy came to the podium.

Manatt grabbed me and said, "What the f*** do you think you are doing?"

I smiled at him and said, "Providing the orchestra you promised me."

I don't think Manatt spoke to me for years.

Ted Kennedy loved the story, and I'm told kept a videotape of the Mummers and his speech in his office for the rest of his career.

I learned that in my personal human nature was a "son of a bitch" quality of playing tough, albeit with a touch of humor. It is said that revenge is a dish that should always be served cold—in this case, it was serenaded in music.

Perils of Legislating

Katherine Rogers

I serve as a state representative in New Hampshire. There are four hundred members of the State House of Representatives and I represent about nine thousand people. I am now in my fifth term; I served previously for four terms.

It has been an interesting experience.

I have been the lead person on a gun violence prevention legislation. Probably the main bill I've worked the hardest on over the years is the background checks for gun purchases. Over the years, I've become the target of stalking and threats by people who like to call themselves "Second Amendment Defenders."

In 2017, I participated in an election recount. In New Hampshire recounts, there are two challengers, one from each side. I was sitting as the challenger for the Democrats and my colleague was the challenger for the Republicans—and a strong gun supporter. When I challenged a particular ballot, she was not happy with that challenge and started to become very loud and animated. I gently put my hands on each side of her face to calm her down. It was uninvited contact, which in New Hampshire can be considered assault. I was wrong and shouldn't have done that. I took my hands off her face and apologized. She became upset and said, "You assaulted me, you touched me, you hit me!"

That was the last I heard of the incident until halfway through the next legislative session.

A Republican legislator had been charged with wrongdoing and the Republicans were looking for a Democrat they could charge as well. At the same time, the woman from the recount incident went to the state police to file assault charges against me. The state police called me, and having been a former prosecutor, I said that I'd rather talk through my attorney. I know better than to talk for myself. I called a friend, probably the best defense attorney in the state, to represent me.

Soon we realized the woman was the president of the Sisters of the Second Amendment. They were very suspicious of the police. A hearing on her complaint was held. She constantly accused the police of being deferential towards me and out to get her. The police were very aware of her organization and fearful that if they didn't come out against me, they would be seen as unfair. They ended up charging me with a Class B misdemeanor for simple assault.

The decision my attorney and I made was that I'd plead guilty to the simple assault, pay the fine, and attend an anger-management evaluation. My accuser was not happy with that result and thought I should be in jail. Actually, she may have thought I deserved the death penalty. I did the anger-management evaluation and it came back saying that it seemed foolish because I didn't have any anger issues.

Since that time, I have faced a few consequences. I had over $2,000 in legal bills because this woman went to the state Bar Association and tried to get me disbarred. She also went to the House Ethics Committee and tried to have me thrown out of the legislature. The process led to a subsequent vote in the House of Representatives. My Republican colleagues supported me, including two of the most right-wing members. Two of the strongest gun supporters told me they were willing to speak on my behalf. In the end, the vote failed.

It was pretty cool to have support from both parties.

One of my other big issues is the humane treatment of animals. It came to my attention that New Hampshire was one of just fourteen states where bestiality was still legal. I was shocked. I thought it was illegal everywhere. In turns out, New

Hampshire was the destination state. People would come here and make bestiality films because it was the only state in New England where it was legal.

The Coalition Against Domestic Violence was going to sponsor this bill because it was a messy issue that no one wanted to talk about. Bestiality was a precursor to domestic violence, sexual violence, child abuse, child violence, pornography, and that sort of thing. It's a natural progression. People who abuse animals most often work up to abusing children and then adults. It is as simple as that.

So, I started the bill and spent a year and a half on it. I would approach people in the Statehouse and begin by saying, "Hey, can I talk to you about bestiality?" It was a real eye-catcher in conversation. They were shocked to see that it was legal.

A hearing was scheduled. It was very unusual. I had to give members print material because there were family members and school kids present. I found a website called beastforum.com. I would never advise anyone to go to because once you see it, there are things that you will never believe. It's very disturbing. It's basically a dating site for people who are into bestiality. People place ads for you to date their pet or pick up a pet to date. It is most common is for dogs. But it has cats and any animal you can think of. I don't think of myself as naive, but I was shocked. You very rarely see legislators be truly shocked. We had an expert from the FBI testify.

We had strong opposition. It amazed me there were people were against outlawing bestiality. The heart of the opposition was the bestiality practitioners. They actually tried to raise money to get an expert from Iran to come speak. Iran? Is Iran a country where bestiality is legal?

The more disturbing opponent was our own Commissioner of Agriculture. She spoke against the bill. I immediately went to the governor. She went ballistic and called the commissioner and said, "What the f*** is your problem? Why are you doing this?"

The commissioner's response was, "Well, this is a slippery slope, once we do this, we won't be able to do artificial insemination."

The governor said, "Are you crazy?"

Unfortunately, both the New Hampshire Farm Bureau and the Dog Owners of New Hampshire (the local chapter of the American Kennel Club) took a stand in support of keeping bestiality legal in the state, claiming it was a "slippery slope." However, more rational groups like the Humane Association of the United States and the local animal shelters and rescue groups came out in strong support of the bill to ban this bizarre practice.

We had a fight on our hands. We were very careful. We talked to animal experts and veterinarians and worded the bill very carefully. That's one thing I found out about legislation—you have to look at every word. We crafted it so it didn't stop artificial insemination and it didn't stop examination by a veterinarian.

I told the Speaker of the House, half-jokingly and half-threateningly, "Look, if there's one speck of opposition to this bill, I'll do a roll call vote—I'll put every Republican on the record."

He replied, "This bill will not be roll called, this will be a fast gavel!"

New Hampshire is no longer the only state in New England where bestiality is legal.

Calling the Shot

Jerry Austin

One of the first campaigns I was involved in was in 1970, when Richard Celeste, who eventually became governor of Ohio, was running for state representative. I was a volunteer driver, and as a driver, I spent a lot of time with the candidate. I got to know the district and a lot of the people who lived there.

The first night we went out to campaign, Dick told me that we were going to end each night campaigning at a local, working-class bar. Dick was a Yale graduate and a Rhodes Scholar, so he wanted people to see he was a real person, not just an egghead.

After that first night of campaigning, we stopped at a bar called Brothers Around on Detroit Avenue in Cleveland. And as we walked in, he told me, "Look, you order either a beer or a beer and a shot. I don't want you ordering any of those New York fizzy drinks, a Whiskey Sour, or a Tom Collins."

I said, "Okay, I understand."

So, we got inside and Dick ordered a beer.

I said, "I'll have a beer and a shot." The bartender looked at me, and I said it again, "I'll have a beer and a shot."

Then Dick said, "Jerry, a shot is not a brand. You have to call a brand."

Well, I never had a shot before, so I thought a shot was a brand. The only brand I know is Jack Daniels.

So, I said, "I'll have a beer and a Jack Daniels."

Dick starts laughing because most people who order a shot order some raw cut, I'm calling out a premier brand.

He said, "Where'd you get Jack Daniels from?"

I said, "Well, Frank drinks Jack Daniels."

He said, "Frank who?"

I said, "Frank Sinatra."

Bloomingdales, Yankee Stadium, and the Supreme Court

Mark Siegel

At the 1976 Democratic National Convention in New York City, Jimmy Carter won a first ballot victory, with almost unanimous support from his native South. His staff, led by campaign manager Hamilton Jordan and pollster/strategist Patrick Caddell, understood that Carter was perceived as a non-establishment moderate and needed an establishment liberal as his running mate. They chose U.S. Senator Walter Mondale of Minnesota.

I was Executive Director of the Democratic National Committee (DNC) and had a long personal and professional relationship with Jimmy Carter, Fritz Mondale, and Hamilton Jordan. I was also a close personal friend of Patrick Caddell.

Shortly after the July convention, former U.S. Senator from Minnesota and liberal icon Eugene McCarthy announced that he planned to run for president as an independent. He would file to get on the ballot in as many states as possible. McCarthy was a hero to liberals because of his early challenge to President Lyndon Johnson over the war in Vietnam. I was concerned about McCarthy's drawing power among liberals, and most especially as it related to my home state (and huge Electoral College prize) of New York.

Carter was not known or popular in New York, with little relationship with the party in the state, its elected officials, its major constituent communities—labor, minorities, Jews, and the academy. Earlier, he had done very poorly in the New York Presidential Primary. Although New York was seen as clearly leaning Democratic and had been carried by Democratic presidential candidates since 1960, I was nervous about New York—especially if there were a major liberal alternative on the ballot like Gene McCarthy.

I shared my concern with Caddell who dove into his data and determined that McCarthy could easily pull up to five-hundred thousand votes from Carter in New York State. Internal polls revealed that McCarthy could receive as much as nine percent of the vote in New York which could throw the state to the Republican nominee, President Gerald Ford.

I told Caddell that there might be a way to knock Gene McCarthy off the ballot in New York. New York election law clearly stipulated the procedures to get a third-party candidate on the ballot. The procedure was burdensome and complicated. It required the signatures of at least twenty-thousand registered Democratic New York voters, and at least fifty voters each from twenty of New York's thirty-nine congressional districts. Furthermore, each signature had to be identified by address, Election District (precinct), Assembly District (state legislative district), and residence at the time of last election.

My own personal experience in New York centered around getting Democratic national convention delegates on the primary ballot, and that experience suggested that the signature gathering process was often haphazard and sloppy. And I was hearing that in New York the McCarthy people were especially disorganized and apparently ignorant of the signature requirements. The McCarthy campaign was setting up tables outside of Bloomingdale's department store on the East Side of Manhattan to get people to sign their petitions as they walked in and out of the department store or passed by on the street. The McCarthy people were actually caught soliciting signatures at Yankee Stadium between innings.

Very frequently people who signed ballot petitions were not registered Democrats. Very few knew their election district or assembly district, and many were not asked for their residence address at the time of the previous election. Without this complicated information, signatures were often found to be invalid. It was reported to me that this kind of sloppy signature collection pattern was taking place all over the state.

The safest and most efficient method to collect valid signatures in New York State was (and still is) to go door-to-door with Democratic registration rolls. McCarthy campaign organizers might have had a lot of experience getting anti-Vietnam war petitions signed on college campuses, but they usually didn't have a clue about New York election law.

I brought the situation to the leadership of Carter's presidential campaign, with my belief that an organized petition challenge effort would likely knock McCarthy off the New York presidential ballot. Caddell agreed with me. He had an internal poll showing Carter at forty-three percent, Ford at forty percent and McCarthy at five percent. We both agreed it was worth the time and money such a petition challenge would cost. It could actually determine not just New York, but in a close election it could determine who would be elected the next president of the United States.

I had worked on complex New York State proportional representation delegate selection issues in 1975 with a brilliant lawyer who served as Counsel to the New York Democratic State Committee, named Melvin Schweitzer. I thought he would be perfect to head a legal challenge to McCarthy's petitions. I also cleared the challenge with Patrick Cunningham, a close friend who was the State Chairman of the New York Democratic Party, who told me the effort would cost at least $40,000.

I then went to my boss, Democratic National Chairman Robert S. Strauss and asked him to authorize the expenditure. Strauss looked at me like I was crazy and said in his inimical Texas drawl: "Son, are you out of your f***ing mind? I'm not going to throw away $40,000 in the middle of a tough campaign on this crazy scheme. You want to do it? You go raise the money."

So, I did. I took up the Strauss challenge. With Caddell and his projected vote charts as an ally and props, I went to Hamilton Jordan and presented the case. He said he never thought of New York as a problem state and asked if McCarthy could really screw up New York. Caddell said that Carter wasn't polling nearly as well with the critical constituencies of Jews and liberals as a Democratic presidential candidate should poll in New York. He said McCarthy could be real trouble for us.

Hamilton authorized the $40,000 expenditure. I contacted the New York Democratic Party Chairman, told him that we were proceeding with the project, and then had the funds transferred. Next, I contact Mel Schweitzer and gave him the green light.

It was a long and complex task. McCarthy had submitted 28,230 signatures on over 3,600 pages. Schweitzer led the legal battle before the State Board of Elections: "In the matter of Gordon Contessa et al. against Eugene J. McCarthy." He had a team of twenty going over the bona fides of each of McCarthy's 28,230 signatures.

As we expected, and as we hoped, the McCarthy effort was sloppy and spotty. Many people who signed were not registered nor Democrats; many omitted the necessary validating information on election districts, assembly districts, and residence at last election. Signature after signature proved to be bogus or lacking backup data. After a long and difficult legal process, 11,720 out of McCarthy's 28,230 signatures were found to be invalid.

McCarthy's lawyers fought hard to keep their candidate on the ballot, challenging decisions by the Board of Election and lower courts that went against them. On October 29, 1976, the highest Court in New York by a vote of 5–2 declared that McCarthy had failed to secure the necessary twenty thousand signatures, and thus could not appear on the New York State presidential ballot.

McCarthy's legal staff made a last desperate attempt to get McCarthy back on the ballot by appealing the decision to the United States Supreme Court. They asked the Court to stay the New York decision and thus put Eugene McCarthy back on the ballot.

Mel Schweitzer had called us at the DNC to ask for our help in representing our position before the Court and getting the necessary filings submitted. We asked the DNC General Counsel Sheldon Cohen (who had been the Director of the Internal Revenue Service in the Johnson Administration) to represent the party before the Supreme Court.

Justice Thurgood Marshall heard the McCarthy appeal. On October 30, Justice Marshall announced his decision and refused to set aside the New York Court order. The ballot challenge petition, after a very long battle, had finally succeeded. Incredibly, the issue was settled only three days before the presidential election.

On November 2, 1976 America voted. Nationally the election was very close, within two points. New York State, as we had feared, was surprisingly close, with Carter winning by a majority of 288,767 votes, well within Caddell's projection of 500,000 votes for McCarthy if McCarthy's name stayed on the ballot. Carter was elected with 297 Electoral votes. If McCarthy had stayed on the ballot in New York and Ford won the state, Gerald Ford would have been elected President with 281 Electoral Votes to Carter's 256.

Liberal columnist James Wechsler wrote, "If McCarthy had not been barred from the New York ballot, President Ford would almost certainly have won the state and the election." Conservative columnist William Safire concurred, "If only the judges of the New York State Court of Appeals had voted differently and kept McCarthy on the ballot he would have received four to five percent of the vote, Ford would have won."

Little things can and often do change history. Threads of human nature—knowledge, experience, intuition, and trust can trigger action. Darker elements like greed, anger, revenge, bitterness, and indifference can create chaos, war, poverty and death. But in this case, sloppy McCarthy campaign staff work in front of Bloomingdales and at Yankee Stadium, triggered a legal petition challenge that went all the way to the Supreme Court of the United States and made Jimmy Carter president.

Without my chutzpah, Caddell's data, Hamilton Jordan's trust, and above all Mel Schweitzer's legal talent, Gerald Ford would have been re-elected president.

As an aside, forty-two years later, over drinks with me in Manhattan, the Honorable Judge Mel Schweitzer was surprised to learn that I had transferred $40,000 to fund the ballot challenge. He thought he was working pro bono.

It seems that the money had disappeared.

Hardball Politics

Evan Dobelle

I was a thirty-three-year-old National Chair of the 1980 Carter/Mondale re-election campaign. Lt. Governor Mario Cuomo and Queens Borough President Donny Manes were our New York campaign co-chairs. We had a drink at the Algonquin Hotel and they told me I needed to get the Brooklyn Democratic Party leader Meade Esposito on board. Meade was close to Mayor Koch, who was not a fan of either Cuomo or Carter.

So, I went to Brooklyn with my young assistant Terry McAuliffe, a future governor of Virginia, whose dad was a Democratic leader in Syracuse. When we entered the Brooklyn party clubhouse, I was ready with my stories about my grandparents who were International Ladies Garment Workers Union members for years and my dad who graduated from Boys High School in Brooklyn.

"The president needs your help," I said.

"Hey kid." Esposito replied, "I hear you're pretty smart. Do you speak Latin?"

"No, I don't."

"Did you ever hear about 'quid pro quo'?"

"I did."

"Good. I want all the federal police working in New York City public housing to come out of the Civil Service and become patronage appointments—all four thousand of them."

"Not happening."

"Well, how about an Italian-American on the Supreme Court, and I don't mean another Cardozo."

"I'm sure the president would seriously consider one if he felt they were qualified."

I could never even imagine how I would have ever asked President Carter for Esposito's requests.

I said, "No," but I understood, as a former mayor (of Pittsfield, Massachusetts), that Esposito felt that those were the rules he grew up with, and his demands weren't unethical.

It was hardball Tammany Hall politics.

At the end of the meeting, I showed respect to him and his organization. The Kennedy people, who were challenging Carter, didn't.

Finally, Rosalyn Carter's appeal at a private lunch along with the legendary former DNC Chair Bob Strauss closed the deal.

Esposito supported us.

Softball Politics

Terry Flemming

I was standing outside of the Ohio Speaker Vern Riffe's office when State Representative Mary Boyle from Cleveland comes running out screaming. I mean she was furious, with a red face. She looked at me and said, "Terry! Can you believe this? They're going to change a congressional district map based on a softball game! Can you believe this?"

"What are you talking about Mary?"

After the 1980 Census, Ohio was redrawing its congressional district lines. State Representative Terry Tranter from Cincinnati was the Democratic point person for congressional redistricting.

Every year the legislators played a softball game and Tranter took it seriously. He would bring his entire family to the game. In the first inning, he hit a single. Then the team manager, Congressman Dennis Eckart from Cleveland, sends in a pinch runner for him. Tranter never plays in the game again.

Tranter went to Speaker Riffe and said he wants to screw Eckart by redrawing his congressional district. The speaker agreed.

Later I asked Vern, "Why did you tell Tranter to go ahead?"

He said, "I have to deal with these idiots every ten years. I don't care who represents Cleveland in Congress. Of course, I told Tranter to go screw Eckart."

Eckart moved and still won the seat in the new district.

"The Right Staff" and "The Amazing Metz"
Dale Butland

There was a lot of bad blood between U.S. Senator John Glenn and Ohio's other U.S. Senator, Howard Metzenbaum. It began with their two primaries against each other. The first was in 1970, when Howard beat John in the primary, and went on to lose the general election to Robert Taft. Then in 1974 when they squared off again. This time, Howard was the incumbent Senator because U.S. Senator Bill Saxby had resigned to become Nixon's Attorney General, and Ohio Governor John Gilligan appointed Howard to that seat until the next election. So John took on the party's endorsed candidate, who at that time was also a sitting U.S. Senator.

It was a knock-down, drag-out primary. There was bad blood from 1970 and it spilled over into 1974. During the course of that campaign, Howard had taken to saying that John had "never held a job before."[*]

At the traditional Cleveland City Club debate held just before the election, John was lying in wait for Howard on the job issue. John gave what's now been called his

---

[*] *According to journalist Tom Diemer: "The suggestion that Metzenbaum accuse Glenn of never having held a job came from the woman who was my editor in my first job after college. I worked for the Lakewood Sun Post. Howard owned the Sun papers chain and my editor was Jean Gerlach. In talking to Howard during that campaign, she said to him something like 'it is so unfair that Glenn is running against you and talking about business when he's never held a job.' It stuck with Howard and he used it to attack Glenn."*

"Gold Star mothers" speech: "I'd like you to go with me to the veterans hospitals of this country, and you look at those young men with their mangled bodies, and you look them in the eye, and tell them that they never held a job. And I want you go with me to the Gold Star mothers of this country, and you look at them, and you tell them that their sons never held a job. I'll tell you Howard Metzenbaum, you should be on your knees every night thanking God that some men in this country held a job."

At that, the Cleveland City Club audience just exploded. The exchange was widely reported, and a few days later, John went on to beat Howard in the primary, then won the general election that fall, and became a U.S. Senator.

Howard followed him into the Senate two years later in 1976. But the bad blood from those previous races lingered. When I joined John's staff in 1980, the two senators were barely on speaking terms and rarely talked to one another. They would work together when they had to, on issues important to Ohio, but, I mean, the softball games between the two Senate office squads in the summertime were something to behold.

Every senatorial staff has a softball team. John's was called the "Right Staff" and Howard's was called "The Amazing Metz." The game between the two offices was a blood sport. I learned when I got there in 1980 that it was the only game all year that both senators would actually show up for and play in themselves. John and Howard regularly accused each other of bringing ringers in to play in the game.

When I joined the staff, I was dragooned into playing on the Glenn softball team. I had once played semi-pro baseball, so I was a pretty good ball player—and certainly good enough to play softball in the Senate league. John told me, "Howard brought in his ringers last year, and I'm thinking about calling Rafer Johnson and Rosie Greer." The former was an Olympian and the latter a professional football player, both of whom John had gotten to know in the 1968 Bobby Kennedy presidential campaign.

That gives you an idea what kind of game this was.

So fast-forward to 1985, about a year after I had become John's press secretary. *The Washington Times,* a right-wing newspaper that was then owned by Reverend Sun Myung Moon, reported on a real estate deal in which Howard had been involved in finding a buyer for one of the major hotels in Washington D.C.—I think it was the Hay Adams.

Well, Howard got a finder's fee for his efforts—and the *Washington Times* just went off on Howard about how unbefitting it was of a senator and so on. But then—in typical *Washington Times* fashion—they wrote an editorial in which they called Howard "an un-reconstructed Stalinist," and brought up his involvement as a young man with the National Lawyers Guild, which the FBI had labeled a "communist front organization." They entitled the editorial, "Senator Metzenbaum's Red Face," which, of course, was a double entendre: suggesting that he was both embarrassed by the hotel deal and that he was also a Communist.

After reading it, I went to John and I said, "Senator, I think you should go to the floor of the Senate and defend Howard."

He looked up and said, "And why would I do that?"

I said, "Well, you should read this."

He reads it—and then said, "I think you're right. Why don't you write a statement for me to read on the floor?"

Just before John left to read the statement, I called Roy Myers, Howard's press secretary at that time. I said, "Roy, I just want you to know that Senator Glenn is going to the floor of the Senate to speak about Howard."

And there this long pause where I know Myer is thinking, "Oh shit, what's he going to say about Howard?"

I said, "I think you'll be pleased."

So John goes to the floor, and he defends Howard in strong terms, saying something like—I'm paraphrasing now—"Howard Metzenbaum and I have had our differences, but he is a loyal American who loves his country and he deserves better than to be attacked with this warmed-over McCarthyism," so on and so forth.

When John got back to our office—he hadn't been back more than five minutes—the phone rang. It was Howard, calling to thank him for what he had done. And that was how the rapprochement between John and Howard occurred.

As a result, when John was up for re-election the next year—1986—Howard volunteered to be John's campaign chairman. And two years later, when Howard was up for re-election in 1988, John returned the favor and became Howard's campaign chairman.

Howard also asked John if he would loan me to him to be his re-election campaign press secretary. John agreed.

I didn't know Howard very well when I went to work for him. But for the first number of months, Howard would fly back to Ohio on weekends. I'd pick him up, and it would just be Howard and me driving around in a car, going to campaign events all over Ohio.

Now when you're cooped up in car for all these hours, you talk about things. And during one of our first weekends together, Peter Harris—who was Howard's campaign manager—told me I should talk with Howard about agreeing to release his tax returns, which he had never done before. Glenn had always released his returns and got a lot of good press out of it.

Of course, Peter and I had seen Howard's returns and they were terrific; he paid a lot in taxes, gave a bundle to charity, and so forth. Peter said, "Well, why don't you take along with you the stuff that you did with John and let Howard read it?"

So, I brought all the press releases and other material we used around the release of John's tax returns and showed them to Howard, who was sitting in the passenger seat as I drove. As Howard was reading through the material, he had his glasses down on his nose in that kind of squint those who knew Howard will remember, and he is talking to himself out loud.

At one point he says, "Christ, Glenn has more money than I do."

I'm driving and didn't even look at Howard when I said, "Yeah, it's not bad for a guy never held a job, huh?"

At that, Howard whipped around to look at me. Then he started to laugh, and said, "You know, that was the dumbest goddamn thing I ever did in politics and John shoved it right up my butt. He beat me with it and I deserved to lose."

Which is when I thought to myself, "Well, this guy and I are going get along. He's got a sense of humor."

Laurel and Hardy

Joanne Limbach

Back in the 1970s, most state legislators in Ohio had a roommate when they came to Columbus because they needed to share expenses. My representative was Bill Hinig and his roommate was representative Art Bowers. Bowers was from a nearby county, and like Hinig, was a veteran. In fact, Hinig had lost a leg in combat. They were quite a pair.

One night, Hinig came home late and Bowers was fast asleep. Hinig started taking the change out of his pockets and made good deal of noise while putting it on the nightstand. Bowers woke up and told him stop it, but Hinig continued emptying his pockets. Then Bowers said, "You are going to be sorry."

When Hinig got up the next morning, he couldn't find his artificial leg. Bowers had taken it and put it outside the back door at the bottom of the stoop. Hopping on one leg from the bedroom all the way through the kitchen and out down the stoop, he picked up his leg. He had a hell of a time coming back up the steps to get back in the house.

Another time Hinig came home, but didn't see Bowers' car in the driveway. Hinig asked, "Where is your car?" Bower replied, "I'm not telling."

Eventually, Hinig pieced the story together. Bowers had a little too much to drink, he probably wrecked his car, and probably found someone to drive him home.

Hinig decided to help Bowers out of the jam. They set the alarm clock for five a.m. They went out to try to find Bower's car before anybody else did. They found the car. They contacted a towing company. The car was towed back home before anyone knew what happened.

Zoo Plane
Joe Slade White

In a campaign, everyone wants to be as close to the candidate as possible—all the time. And you can measure the power of someone on a campaign plane by the inches away that person sits from the candidate. If you're sitting too far away, you don't count. If you're sitting right next to the candidate, you are the most powerful. You will always know what's going on; you'll hear every conversation; and if necessary, you can head off anyone who would *like* the candidate's ear. I'm not saying knife fights have broken out over proximity, but pretty close.

In fact, my roommate on the 1972 presidential campaign, John Gage, came across a book that was an eighteenth-century firsthand account of the court surrounding French King Louis XV. Even then, courtiers measured their favor and power by minuscule increments of inches of how close they were allowed to be from the throne.

In the front of the plane in the 1972 McGovern presidential campaign, there were two sets of seats facing each other so that conversations could take place easily. The candidate had the window seat, facing forward. The first most powerful person had the seat next to the candidate. The next most powerful spot was the chair facing the candidate, and finally, the third most powerful, was the person facing the back of the plane on the aisle. And who sat where depended on who was on any given trip.

I was just a twenty-one-year-old kid at the time. My job was to tape everything George McGovern said, whether it was a simple statement, a speech before thousands of people in an arena, or a press conference (that's what they were called back then). The journalists covering the campaign included all the press, even if they were reporting for CBS or NBC or the *New York Times* or the *Washington Post*. After taping things, I would hook up my tape recorder to a phone line and send the clips I thought were the most important for the campaign to distribute to radio stations across the nation, especially to targeted areas and primary states.

People ask me how I got the job and it was simple. I walked into the McGovern headquarters and asked for a job. I was interviewed by Frank Mankiewicz, the co-campaign manager with Gary Hart, and George Cunningham, McGovern's chief of staff. They handed me a portable cassette tape recorder and I went to work devising a plan for a network of high school and college kids who would get up at five every morning and call the radio stations in their states or regions to offer them actual sound of McGovern from the day before, saying something newsworthy (one hoped) from wherever in the country he was campaigning.

There was no cable TV back then. There were only three national television networks, NBC, CBS, and ABC. Fox Broadcasting didn't exist. And all three networks had one or two correspondents traveling with a presidential campaign, along with a film crew shooting the news footage on 16mm film. Portable video tape had not yet been invented. Small planes owned by the networks would meet the campaign plane at whatever airport we ended up at the end of the night, and through the night they would fly the undeveloped film back to New York so that it could be processed, edited, and aired the next day or in the traditional nightly national newscasts.

What started out as four of us plus the candidate flying around New Hampshire and Wisconsin during the early primaries, soon became two large Boeing 727 passenger jets leased from United Airlines.

The main plane held the candidate, the top staff, and the stars of the press—the top network correspondents, the top political journalists, plus any state and local politicians who were being courted for endorsements and support. The second plane was called the "Zoo Plane," an affectionate term for the plane that held the lesser of us on the campaign's staff and network correspondents, plus political reporters who were slightly junior to their more recognized colleagues on any given newspaper.

What soon became apparent was that the Zoo Plane had more fun. We weren't constrained by the presence of the candidate, senior campaign officials, nor the demi-gods of network television, newspapers, and magazines. There was a comradery of being "second best." And often the top reporters and network correspondents would trade off with their "lesser" associates at the same newspaper, network, or magazine, so that they could ride on the Zoo Plane.

Ironically, given what I said about proximity, the Zoo Plane became coveted. We each had first-class seats in rows of four across. There was a lot more laughter and probably a little more drinking. It was possible to sit in the jump seat in the cockpit during a take-off or a landing, which I'll never forget, and few people will ever experience.

There was not the suspicion and ill feelings that one senses today between campaigns and journalists. We got to know each other. We knew our jobs weren't always in sync, but we respected each other and enjoyed each other's company and stories. I was in awe. I knew and know now how incredibly lucky I was. I met legends and those who would become legends.

Forty years later I was asked to create a documentary about the campaign to honor Senator George McGovern on the anniversary of his presidential nomination and his birthday. The event was to take place in Washington D.C. So, I set about to write a script and to assemble footage and still photographs that had been taken by two other twenty-somethings in 1972 who traveled and documented the campaign, Stuart Bratesman and Keith Wessel.

One day while we were working on the documentary, a young junior staff person in my firm came running up to me all excited and said, "Oh Mr. White. I didn't know you were on the McGovern campaign. You must have known—" I expected her to say, Senator McGovern, Gary Hart or Frank Mankiewicz, but no, she said, "Hunter Thompson." I smiled and said, "Yep." And thought to myself, well, she's right. Knowing Hunter Thompson was unique.

Jann Wenner, the publisher of *Rolling Stone*, brilliantly figured that it was time for something new when it came to reporting on a presidential campaign. It would appear weekly, not daily. Wenner could give the pieces a lot of space and he knew just who would be perfect: Hunter S. Thompson. Thompson had already achieved notoriety for a book that was a firsthand account of the Hell's Angels. But he wasn't yet well known and most national political journalists didn't have the slightest idea of who he was.

Hunter showed up one day to board the Zoo Plane: a tall, balding young man, wearing yellow aviator sunglasses, vintage shirts from the 1950s and polyester slacks in alarming colors, while smoking cigarettes non-stop with a distinctive ivory cigarette holder. People didn't know what to make of him. Some were alarmed. Most of us were fascinated. The establishment reporters didn't know what to do.

But within a matter of two or maybe three weeks, reporters for the top media organizations were running off the planes to get to the airport's newsstand to grab the latest issue of *Rolling Stone* to see what Hunter had written *that* week. It was like witnessing a sea change or an earthquake in political journalism. It was personal; it was brilliant; it was at times outrageous; always insightful; and no matter how outrageous, it was always the truth as Hunter S. Thompson saw it, heard it, and smelled it. It was also beautifully written and powerful.

Later, many of Hunter's articles appeared in *Fear and Loathing: On the Campaign Trail '72*. And Hunter's assistant, Tim Crouse, wrote a wonderful book about the life of journalists on the campaign trail entitled *The Boys on the Bus*.

Yes, I was lucky that Hunter Thompson was first assigned to the Zoo Plane. He liked the atmosphere, and stayed, even when he was offered an upgrade to the candidate's plane. Thompson and McGovern got along wonderfully. Thompson, born and raised in Louisville, Kentucky, and George McGovern, born and raised in Mitchell, South Dakota, respected each other. Both understood they were fighting to change the worlds they worked in, journalism and government, respectively. While others at the time saw those changes as radical and threatening, to Hunter S. Thompson and George McGovern, well, they just made perfect sense.

Carter, Mineta, and Me

Les Francis

A post-1976 election memo that I wrote to my then boss, Congressman Norm Mineta, argued that he and his congressional peers who were elected in 1972, 1974, and 1976 could form a natural political foundation for the newly elected President Carter. That memo ultimately found its way to Vice President Mondale, then Frank Moore, and before long I was soon working in the West Wing. There was no plan hatched, no serious plotting—it was all just dumb luck.

Once in the White House, and although brought in as a "Carter guy," I developed excellent relations with Mondale's staff. And I gradually got to know and become friendly with the vice president himself. He would see me in his outer office and say something like, "Hey Les, come on in. What do you hear?" We'd chat about the latest political news or happenings on Capitol Hill. I was invited to travel with Mondale whenever he went to California, either on "official business" or for political purposes.

One traveling experience with the vice president was memorable, but not pleasant. In the summer of 1979 Mondale was dispatched to speak, first to the American Federation of Teachers (AFT) Convention in San Francisco and then to Detroit to make a similar address to the rival National Education Association (NEA) Representative Assembly. I was asked to go along for a couple of reasons. First, California was my political responsibility and I traveled there whenever Carter or Mondale did. Second, I was responsible for maintaining the administration's ties to NEA (which would be a critical ingredient in our fight for re-nomination and re-election).

The AFT event was likely not going to be as pleasant, because the union opposed the administration's drive to create a cabinet-level Department of Education, while the NEA was its foremost advocate.

Flying first to San Francisco, the vice president's office—appropriately—had invited the late Representative Phil Burton (whose congressional district Nancy Pelosi now represents) to hitch a ride home on Air Force Two. The landing gear had barely been retracted when Burton started drinking double vodkas and milk. As he drank, Burton became more, I think the word is "assertive." Sitting up front in Mondale's cabin, drinking a prodigious amount (by the time we landed Burton had consumed fourteen of such concoctions by the stewards' count), Burton got more and more agitated and angry—at the Carter administration in general, and at me in particular.

At some point in the journey, the vice president looked down the aisle, beckoned for me to come up front and sit with him. Burton went on and on about what a jerk Jimmy Carter was. I was just as bad—maybe worse. All sorts of terms were used to describe the president and me (as his chief California political liaison), but as I recall "mother f***er" and "cock s***ker" were among his favorites that morning.

Burton's views toward Carter, although perhaps more colorfully phrased, were not unlike those of others on the labor/liberal left of the Democratic Party. Carter was a true centrist: liberal on civil liberties, civil rights, international human rights, and environmental matters, but he was conservative on fiscal matters. He was also downright skeptical toward many liberal prescriptions on domestic issues. As I've noted in multiple papers and talks, Carter's was a transitional presidency, both for the institution itself as well as for his party.

My problems with Phil Burton—or more correctly, his problems with me—were much less consequential, but no less bitter. First, he didn't trust me because of my ties to Congressman Norm Mineta, who he believed—incorrectly, it must be noted—had voted against him in the Majority Leader's race in 1976 (which he lost by a single vote). Despite assurances to the contrary from Norm and others, Phil went to his grave thinking that Norm had sabotaged his leadership ambitions. So, he figured that if Norm had screwed him, so had I!

His belief in that vein was reinforced when one of my colleagues on the White House staff recounted a story to Phil which was true, but which should not have been shared beyond the confines of the West Wing.

At one meeting of the congressional liaison staff, a matter relating to California—I cannot remember what it was exactly—was discussed. During the course of the conversation someone suggested that before the administration did anything on the subject, we should run it by Phil "because he controls politics in California." I took exception to that characterization, explaining that the politics of California were much more complex than that, and that while Burton certainly had statewide influence, driven in part by his alliance with Congressmen Henry Waxman and Howard Berman in Los Angeles, it was simply not true that he "ran" California politics. Moreover, I went on to argue that even in his home city of San Francisco, Burton's power was not exactly complete, and I cited as proof the fact that Dianne Feinstein (who, as I recall, had recently become mayor after the assassination of George Moscone) was anything but a Phil Burton toady. Well, that discussion had barely ended when someone who had been involved retold it to Burton, who—not surprisingly—went ballistic.

So, aboard Air Force Two, with the vice president as a captive audience and me a hapless witness, Burton summoned up all his outrage at Carter, Mineta, and me. He would bang his glass of vodka, milk, and ice on his armrest to emphasize a particular point, and the contents flew—like the expletives—in all directions!

I was mortified. Mondale, on the other hand, loved the whole scene. He simply thought the display was so bizarre that it was just plain funny. He has since laughed with me many times as he recounted the story to others.

Good Morning, Palm Beach
Kevin Lampe

I'm doing advance work for Vice President Al Gore. We are down in Florida. Kitty Kurth, my wife, is the lead for the vice president, and I'm the site person for the fundraising event of Al Gore's trip.

President Clinton was planning to attend the event. But because of the looming government shutdown, it was decided just days before the event that the president would not be joining us in Palm Beach, Florida. So, the presidential advance team starts bugging out. We head quickly over to the hotel and ask them to leave us some assets. Now, in that day you needed a fax machine, walkie-talkies, and so forth. We also asked to have a couple of people from the president's team to join our team so we could have a full team.

We find out that there's going to be an OTR, which means an "off the record event." Al Gore is going to attend a Simchat Torah service with the host of the fundraiser.

We find out that we need to talk with the Rabbi. The Rabbi is there with his father-in-law, and we think, "Gosh, this father-in-law, what does he want? He just wants to be a part of this."

We're discussing with the Rabbi about everything that is going to happen at the services that Vice President Al Gore may attend. We always say "may attend"—no promises. We get into the details of the visit. The father-in-law is asking a lot of questions and really trying to be a part of everything that's going on.

So, we get back to our hotel and we have our countdown meeting. It turns out that someone at the White House had placed the visit on the official schedule, which then meant the Secret Service had to visit the site—the Secret Service is in a panic. I'm like, "Wait, there's a service going on right now at the temple. We need to go back, and we need to be very careful. We will go in two cars. I will go ahead, you come in the second car, and when I can connect with the Rabbi, then we will do the security check that we need to do."

So, we get to the temple. It's the night before the Simchat Torah service, and the Rabbi is in the middle of the street dancing with the Torah. Everyone is around him. It is pandemonium. Singing and shouting: a big celebration is going on, a big party. I can't make my way to the Rabbi. But who do I see? I go over to his father-in-law. I later learned, he's a big shot lawyer with one of the biggest law firms. He's on the board of The Nature Conservancy. He is a real player that I actually should know.

The father-in-law takes us all around the temple. We meet the "alter kakers," the old guys who really run the temple. They're excited about Gore being there. They tell us, "Now, there's a couple of guys here at the temple, they don't like the Clintons." And they go, "Could we give you their pictures?" Secret Service says, "Yes, please give us their pictures."

We go around everywhere. The "alter kakers" ask, "Oh gosh. Where are the dogs? Are the bomb dogs going to come? We want everybody to be safe here. This is going to be wonderful." We do the security check. We toured all around the temple. And then, after we finished the tour, we go back to where the big party is still going on.

The Secret Service agents and I finally talk to the Rabbi. He's thrilled, he's so excited, and he says, "Oh, all of us, we should do a shot of vodka together." Now, none of us wants to offend our hosts, so we agree to partake. The Rabbi teaches us the Russian way of doing a shot of vodka, which involves pumpernickel, pickle, and vodka—it is all a grand, wonderful ceremony. We do the shot of vodka and go back to our hotel. I don't think this shot is a big thing. I send my briefing off to the White House. Everything is ready at the temple.

The next morning the temple is our first stop after a quick press conference at the airport. I'm there to greet the car when it pulls up. We enter into services. Gore is going to sit on the Bema, on the altar in the temple. I'm sitting next to one of the "alter kakers," who actually asked me, "Are you Jewish, young man?" And I say, "Oh, no. I'm Catholic." He goes, "Ah, you could pass." He goes on, "I'll explain everything to you."

So, this fine gentleman is explaining to me everything that's going on during the service. Everything is smooth. The Rabbi gets up. He introduces the vice president. He says, "Oh, I can't believe I'm going to introduce the vice president who will be president someday but not so soon."

The Rabbi, he tells this moving story about his fight for freedom in USSR, and how on his last night he in Moscow, he gets kicked out of his favorite restaurant for speaking Hebrew. An emotional civil rights story.

The Rabbi then introduces Al Gore, and the vice president approaches the podium. He starts to shift his weight and I find out he's a little nervous. He begins the speech. Then he goes on and it's going fine. And then Gore says to the congregation, "Oh, and last night I heard you had a great party." And the Rabbi interrupts him and says, "Oh, Mr. Vice President, you think last night was a party. Now, it's a party." He reaches behind his chair next to the table and pulls out vodka, pumpernickel, a pickle, and shot glasses.

I'm like, "Oh my God, this is not going to go well. I had not told the vice president there was going to be shots of vodka during the services."

The Rabbi takes the tray to the vice president, who grabs for the shot and tries to start drinking. The Rabbi says, "Oh no, no, no, no. Let me show you how to do it." The Rabbi says, "First, Mr. Vice President, you must relax your shoulders."

So, the vice president says, "For years, people have been telling me to do that." They worked through the whole ceremony of the pumpernickel and the pickle, and then turning around, the shot of vodka. The vice president says, "I'm much more relaxed now."

Then Gore said, "That reminds me of a story of the first Jewish president of the United States."

I'm thinking, "Oh my God, where's the vice president going? This is going to be terrible. He's probably telling the wrong joke to the wrong group of people. I'm going to go down in history just like the other advance people who put Dukakis in the helmet, who put Bob Dole on that stage he fell off of, and who got Gore drunk at ten a.m. in Palm Beach."

Gore then starts the story. The story goes like this:

The first Jewish president calls his mom and says, "Mom, you must come to the inauguration."

She goes, "Oh my son, I don't know. It's going to be too cold."

"Mom, I'll buy you a warm coat."

"Oh, but I have nothing to wear."

"Mom, I will get you a wonderful dress."

"Oh, okay. But, son, I have nobody to talk to."

"Mom, I'll sit you next to the new Secretary of State. He's a nice man. You'll get along."

"All right, I will come."

The first Jewish president is being sworn in, and just as he's being sworn in, his mother turns to the Secretary of State, points to her son, and says, "You see that young man down there? His brother is a doctor."

Crowd cracks up. Everybody's laughing. The old guy next to him goes, "I love that story. What a wonderful story."

I'm so relieved. We finished the trip.

Later I find out from Gore that the story had always been a part of the speech. He just didn't know when he was going to be able to tell it. The look that he gave me was not the look I thought that was going to get me fired, but it was a look of, "This is okay, Kevin."

But that was the day that I watched Al Gore do a shot of vodka in a temple in Palm Beach during the morning.

The Governor is Gay

Hank Sheinkopf

A New Jersey friend calls. It's the middle of the summer and it's hot as hell. He says, "Hank, our governor's gay and he's coming out of the closet at a four p.m. press conference. His lover is trying to extort $50 million from him not to go public. I need you in Princeton, New Jersey, in an hour."

That's not a call you get every day. But I'm crisis PR guy and I had handled disasters like this one all the time.

I get on the road from New York City. I arrive at the New Jersey governor's mansion and the state police waved me in. I get inside and go to the library where Governor McGreevy, his staff, and political consultants are meeting.

I wasn't a consultant to the governor, so I asked why he called me. The governor said he trusted my judgment and my reputation with the press has always been particularly good.

The governor looks at me and says, "Well Hank, what do you think we should do?"

I said, "Governor, let's do nothing until we get some information. I wanted to hear your lover's story and the source of his problem."

I spend an hour hearing information about the lover.

Then I said, "Governor, we're certainly announcing your resignation. If you do not announce your resignation, you'll be impeached."

He said, "Ok. I think I'll leave December 31st."

I said, "I don't think so. My advice to you is that you leave sooner than later."

"When?"

"You cannot be in the governor's mansion over Thanksgiving weekend with your infant child and your wife that you cheated on. It's just not going to work. The stories will overwhelm you."

"Ok, what's the date?"

I picked a date. I had no idea what the constitutional implications were in the State of New Jersey.

I said, "We've got to move."

I got him on the phone with the FBI. He used the phrase, "This is an attempted extortion."

"You think this is going be a big story?" I said, "I've been at this work a few years. I think this is going to be a major story, a big international story."

"Are you sure?"

"My experience tells me that this is going to be very big."

"Are you sure?"

"Here it is: 'Top of the six news. New Jersey's governor is gay. Back after this.'"

"Are you sure?"

"I'm positive."

I was right.

V. Personalities

Why Not, Barack?

Kitty Kurth

On April 3, 1996, the United States Secretary of Commerce, Ron H. Brown, was killed in a plane crash near Dubrovnik, Croatia. In addition to Secretary Brown, I had several other friends on board who died that day.

I was in my office in Chicago overlooking Michigan Avenue. I could not stop crying. I was thinking about the young political operatives whose lives were cut short and thinking about Ron Brown who I had liked and admired so much.

I first met Ron at the Democratic Convention in Atlanta in 1988 when he was helping Reverend Jesse Jackson negotiate with the Dukakis for President Campaign. His diplomatic and communications skills were marvelous to watch. His charisma won him friends and admirers everywhere he went.

He was elected chair of the Democratic National Committee (DNC) in February of 1989. I had traveled around the country helping him meet and sway Democrats all over the country. Brown used his charm and eloquence on the leaders of the Mormon Church in Salt Lake City and the hardboiled Chicago Democratic Party stalwarts alike. You could tell he would be a rising star in the Democratic stratosphere for decades to come.

Under Brown, the DNC was stronger than it had ever been. More people felt included and energized. The invigorated party helped Bill Clinton win the presidency in 1992. Clinton appointed Brown as Secretary of Commerce, the perfect job for Brown to use both his business connections and political skills.

When I heard he died, I felt like it was the death of the Democrat's future. I had had such high hopes for Ron's future in electoral politics or wherever he wanted to go. I felt like everything was lost when I heard that the plane crashed.

Later that same day, I had a previously scheduled appointment with a young politico who was running for office for the first time in Chicago. I first met him when he was a volunteer on a congressional campaign with which I was consulting. He had been part of the kitchen cabinet and wrote issue papers for the campaign.

He wanted advice on running for office. He had secured the nomination for state senator from my area and wanted to know who to meet, how to raise money, and who to cultivate for support in my neighborhood.

As he arrived at our office, he came in and his eyes soaked in all of our old campaign memorabilia that covered the walls, the bookshelves, and the bulletin boards. Then he looked at me and asked me why I was crying.

I explained that it was for so many reasons. I was crying for my friends on the plane, crying for Ron's family, crying for Ron. And crying for the country who had lost a leader. I told him I was crying because I had really wanted to work for Ron for vice president someday. (I was thinking of a future Gore-Brown ticket.)

I finally stopped crying and looked at him. I said, "Maybe I can work for you for vice president someday."

He looked back at me and said, "Why not president?" I looked at him and realized that this was a joke that was not a joke.

I thought about it for a minute, thought about him, thought about his wife, and I said, "Why not, Barack?"

Barack Obama and I talked for a while longer, about health insurance in America and other issues. His mother had died recently. He was sad and frustrated that his mother had to spend the last years of her life fighting with insurance companies, rather than focusing on her health.

We talked some more, about other presidents and how young they were when they started thinking about running for the White House and the things they did to start their paths to victory.

Finally, we got around to what he had come to talk with me about, advice and counsel for his campaign to be state senator—my state senator.

He asked me to introduce to him to David Axelrod. I said that I knew David but David wouldn't work with someone who was only running for State Senate. David's clients were U.S. senators, congressmen, and big city mayors. I told him we needed somebody more important than me to introduce him to Axelrod, so that Ax would pay attention.

I suggested that I first introduce Barack to Bettylu Saltzman, an influential Democratic donor and operative. Axelrod would listen to her, and better yet, she lived in the district that Barack was running to represent.

It worked. I introduced Barack to her, she introduced Barack to Axelrod. And the rest, as they say, is history.

Dick Morris
Hank Sheinkopf

I met Dick Morris for the first time in 1982, introduced by a phone guy. Phone guys did canvas calls and persuasion calls. Dick was a name partner in a firm with total campaign service vendors in a single suite. They polled and also did media buying for political campaigns. He and his partners were salesmen. They resided in New York, but really lived on the road, selling and servicing clients. They worked for Republicans and Democrats. We together worked on a lot of campaigns.

I had never met anybody as smart, fast, or different as Dick Morris. His brain moved in a very unique way. He was obsessive. He would buy paper airline tickets by the stack, which was the way it was done in those days. He'd rip off a ticket from that stack every time he needed one as often as three times a day. His wristwatch was a stopwatch and it told him the exact amount of time it would take for him to get back to the airport as well as the length of an ad. The man lived in the air. In every airport he had a system—no cell phones, but payphones—to convince anyone who needed a nudge that his calls couldn't wait. He ran his office out of a pocket old-style Sharp computer, billing scheduling, call list, and everything else.

Less than a year after we met, Dick calls. "Meet me tomorrow morning at eight a.m. in East Orange, New Jersey for a mayoral race," he says. I get to the address. The door opens. You can't go into the apartment until you take off your shoes. No protest allowed. The guy telling you "socks only" has a forty-five-caliber automatic pistol in a shoulder holster. He's tall, muscled, and Black.

Morris is sitting on the floor, another fellow next to him, and the apartment owner is sitting in the center of the room. Purposefully well spoken, the man with the bodyguard is referred to as Mr. Fields. The candidate shows up. We do the work. He wins. Mr. Fields and the new mayor both get grabbed up and go to jail. I never wanted to know why.

Later, Dick calls: "Meet me in Jackson, Mississippi, tomorrow." I go to Memphis, fly to Atlanta, and hop on a flight to Jackson. The heated mist comes out of the ground during the summer day that time of year, giving off this smoky hot smell. I arrive at the meeting and I'm out there looking just like a Yankee with a suit and tie on. Out of the mist comes Dick in a wool suit, which was amazing in that weather. Think he was wearing rattlesnake skin shoes, with a tie on, and he didn't skip a beat. He just started talking and said how a chief of staff to a state senator wanted to become state treasurer. In an hour or less, the ads were written, approved, and a date to shoot them was set. I learned about the Mississippi political mafia, a lot of whom wound up doing time in federal prisons. But they loved Dick.

Dick was always polling. Some people questioned his polls. A lot of people believed he made the polls up. He might have. His polls might not make sense to some, but that didn't matter. He would come up with a hundred ideas at a rapid-fire pace: two would be good, ninety-eight not so good, but the two that were good were really good. His good ideas worked and he could just talk the ears off a dog. He saw things very few could see.

I saw his polling for the first time in the state treasurer campaign. He did this poll with a lot of paragraphing. He asked voters what they felt about depositing state sales tax payments in local banks instead of using the U.S. Postal Service. Then Mississippians would be able, Dick wrote, to earn interest on their sales tax bank deposits, which could be used to build schools and roads.

Then we wrote ads. I put up a boom mic and a camera on a block and started asking people, "What would you do if you had three million dollars more?" It just was a random number. One said they would buy a house, another said they would help their grandchildren. One said, "I'd take a vacation." The candidate for state treasurer looked at the camera and said, "I'd build schools and build roads." It worked. The candidate won.

Toward the end of our relationship, he hired me to work on President Bill Clinton's re-election campaign. I shot the first ads. Morris' polling had Clinton down by as much as thirty-five points. A Wednesday night meeting in the White House upstairs residence library, the menu was water and Morris. Morris was just the most amazing orator. I later learned he had gone to Columbia on a sports scholarship and the sport was debating. He's explaining that if we don't start spending money now, in January 1995, seventeen months before the election, Clinton and Gore would be looking for other work along with those at the meeting who were on the White House payroll. Some people might say this event didn't happen, but I was there to witness it and it did happen.

Morris looks at Clinton, stands up and said: "Mr. President, if we don't spend $10–$15 million on television this year, you're going to lose."

Bill Clinton looked up at Morris and said, "You know what Dick, if we don't spend $10–$15 million this election on television, we're going to lose the election."

Al Gore said, "If we don't spend $10–$15 million this year on television, we're going lose this election."

Harold Ickes, the campaign director, looked at us like we were nuts. That was a lot of money in those years, and there were serious legal questions in those years about spending in the year before the election. He hated Dick Morris.

We raised and spent the money. We changed the law in such a way that it ultimately created the independent expenditure feeding frenzy we have today.

Be Kind to Dogs — and Vote Democratic
Les Francis

After starting my own communications and public affairs firm in 1981, and endeavoring to develop a corporate services practice, I continued to be active in Democratic political circles, including some campaign consulting work.

In 1982, I was asked by Leon Billings, who was the Executive Director of the Democratic Senatorial Campaign Committee (DSCC), at the time, to help with one of that year's key races—the fight between New Mexico's Republican incumbent Harrison "Jack" Schmidt and his Democratic challenger, then-State Attorney General Jeff Bingaman.

Bingaman had won a tough primary election, but Leon and members of the DSCC were worried about the campaign's ability to wage an effective effort against a well-financed incumbent. Leon, as a result, asked me to make an initial "fact-finding" trip to the state, to assess the campaign's strengths and weaknesses, and to report back to him and to then-Senator Thomas Eagleton of Missouri, who had been assigned to be Bingaman's "buddy" among incumbent Senate Democrats.

I made a couple of trips to the state, and met with various campaign aides, party leaders and others including fellow Carter-era campaign veterans Tim Kraft and Chris Brown, both of whom lived in New Mexico. I also attended a two-day campaign "retreat" with Jeff and his team, where we went through the general election plan step-by-step.

After that session, and before I headed back to Washington D.C., Jeff asked if I would be willing to shift from being a consultant/adviser provided by the DSCC to taking over as his campaign manager, the role of which was being filled by an old friend and colleague of Jeff's, Reese Fullerton. I had grown to like and respect Reese a great deal, so on a personal level I was reluctant to see him moved aside. Nevertheless, I shared Jeff's view that he might not have the background or demeanor necessary to manage what was going to be a very tough, high profile, U.S. Senate campaign.

When I got back to Washington D.C., I met with Billings and Senator Eagleton to give them an update, and to discuss Jeff's proposal. They thought it was an excellent idea. I turned around almost immediately and flew back to Albuquerque, took up residence at Santa Fe's La Posada Hotel, and took over the management reins of the campaign. Importantly, Reese Fullerton not only accepted the change, he embraced it, and proved to be a terrific ally and wise counsel to me throughout the fall. It was truly a class act.

Ultimately, Bingaman won by about fifty-four to forty-six percent, the only Democrat to defeat an incumbent Republican Senator during that cycle. That made the campaign a very satisfying experience as well as one that enhanced my credentials as a Democratic operative.

But it was a memorable experience for other reasons, as a couple of highlights will attest.

Not long after arriving in the state to take over the campaign, I called my old friend Carl Wagner, who had a well-earned reputation as one of the very best field organizers the Democratic Party has ever seen. I told him what I was up to, and I asked if he'd be willing to come out to New Mexico and put together our Get Out the Vote (GOTV) operation. Without a moment's hesitation, Carl responded in the affirmative, reinforcing again my belief in the importance of friendships and loyalty in politics.

I also was exposed to what I and others believe is the devious and offensive nature of the now infamous Dick Morris, who Jeff had used a bit in the primary, and whose advice he sought late in the general after Schmitt launched a wave of horrible (and as it turned out totally inaccurate) negative TV ads. Morris did some tracking polls at Jeff's request and advised him to respond with equally harsh negative ads. Because I was highly suspicious of Morris' poll numbers, and even more skeptical of his recommendations, I asked Chris Brown to also do some polling so we could compare his data with Morris'.

After comparing the results, Carl, Chris, and I were convinced we had been on the right track, and what Morris was recommending would not help and ran the real risk of backfiring. So, instead of following Morris' advice, we created some very credible third-party "testimonials" (including one particularly powerful TV spot by the Catholic Archbishop) to refute Schmitt's bogus allegations and testify to Jeff's character and experience. The result was just what we wanted, as undecided voters began to break heavily in Jeff's direction in the final days of the campaign.

But without a doubt, the best fringe benefit of working on that campaign was getting to know Senator Tom Eagleton better, and to become one of "Eagleton's guys." I had always admired the Senator from afar, starting when he was run through the wringer in the 1972 presidential campaign. He was picked to be George McGovern's running mate at the Miami convention only to be yanked from the ticket after it was disclosed he had been treated for clinical depression years before. How he handled that episode—with real grace and courage—said many more positive things about Tom Eagleton than it did negative ones.

Over the next couple of decades, I was honored and privileged to earn Tom Eagleton's personal friendship and professional association (as he brought me into Missouri to run a couple of successful ballot measure campaigns). We enjoyed a few meals together, more than a few drinks, and a couple of St. Louis Cardinals baseball games. I was terribly saddened when I learned of Tom's passing in 2007, but his last written public words are wonderful to remember and make me smile every time I read them: "Go forth in love and peace—be kind to dogs—and vote Democratic."

Roger Stone
Hank Sheinkopf

I met Roger Stone in 1983. I knew him and Paul Manafort. They were outsiders and I was an outsider since I didn't live in Washington D.C. and had no desire to. I wanted to do campaigns that others didn't want to do in places that others didn't want to go to. I was more comfortable in Montgomery, Alabama than I was in Silver Spring, Maryland.

Stone was stylish, which I had never seen in consultants before. He had an impact on how I wanted to carry myself and dress. He was serious—and outrageous. He was a character, but he knew how things fit together. He also had a very decisive personality.

He was fascinating to me because he and his partners understood what Democrats were supposed to do, but stopped doing. The end result was that they won many more elections than other guys. Stone and his partners, like Paul Manafort, were different Republicans. They weren't Park Avenue. They were shit-kickers, and they were Republicans acting like Democrats should act in elections. Stone was one tough guy, tough and smart.

So we had lunch for the first time in 1983, and we ended up working in some campaigns in South Jersey. We also worked for gaming companies in the deep South on pro-gambling ballot measures. He hired me in 1996 on a Florida statewide ballot initiative. Roger was the general strategist. He came back from a sixty-point deficit and ended up winning the thing.

Stones' sense of timing was extraordinary. He believed you went on the attack and didn't stop. You continued being aggressive throughout a campaign. Once you opened a wound—and he understood boxing better than I ever could—you kept banging the wound until there's blood all over the ring.

Roger hired me to work in the late 1990s on a Donald Trump-related campaign. Trump and Stone were very tight, a dynamic duo. Stone always said that Trump would be president someday. People thought he was nuts.

But that Trump, and the Trump in the White House, are like two strangers. That Trump was calm, direct, almost aloof, not overly aggressive, not overly crazy. Trump's office was something else, but I have never been impressed by fancy offices. I wanted to get the money he owed me and get back on the road to the next campaign. Instead, Trump offered me U.S. Open tickets and flights to Palm Beach to go see relatives. I don't think he meant anything by it.

I told him that I don't want any of that, I just want my money.

He paid.

How Not to Make a Deal
Mark Siegel

In March of 1988, the Westin hotel chain sold New York's iconic Plaza Hotel to Donald Trump for $390 million. Trump tasked his then-wife Ivana with decorating and restoring the hotel to its historic elegance. The following year Benazir Bhutto embarked on an "official visit" to the United States. As head of government, this trip could not be called a "state visit" because the figurehead President of Pakistan was officially the head of state, similar to Queen Elizabeth II in the United Kingdom.

After what was considered a triumphant two-day visit to Washington, D.C. highlighted by a speech before a Joint Session of the U.S. Congress and a glittery dinner in the White House, the Prime Minister traveled to Boston where she delivered the Commencement Speech at Harvard University and received an honorary doctorate. She left Boston for New York where she spoke before the Asia Society and attended a reception in her honor at the Plaza Hotel.

The reception at the Plaza Hotel was hosted by Donald and Ivana Trump and was attended by much of New York's social, economic, and political glitterati. I organized the official visit in all three cities and therefore worked with Trump's representatives on the logistics of the Prime Minister's soiree at the Plaza Hotel. I met Ivana and Donald Trump at the reception. Benazir introduced me to them as her friend and the man who handled her affairs in the United States. It was a beautiful and elegant affair, and I thought that would be the last of my dealings with Donald Trump.

I was wrong.

Shortly after Benazir returned to Pakistan, I received a call at my office in Washington D.C. from Donald Trump's scheduler asking if I would be available to meet with Trump. I asked what the purpose would be and was told it was a matter that he wished to discuss with me privately. One week later I flew to New York and went to Trump Tower on Fifth Avenue. I was ushered into Trump's elaborate office on a high floor with a commanding view of the city. Trump was alone. He greeted me warmly and thanked me for coming. We chatted for a bit about inconsequential things and I thanked him for his hospitality to Benazir at the Plaza.

After a few minutes, I said, "Well Mr. Trump, you asked me to come to New York, what would you like to talk about?"

He said, "Call me Donald."

I said "OK, Donald, so why am I here?"

He said, "Mark, I understand that you control Benazir Bhutto."

I laughed out loud and responded, "Donald, no one controls Benazir."

He said, "Well, I'm told that she listens to everything you say."

I laughed again and said, "Sure, she listens to everything I say, about ten percent of the time."

Donald Trump then told me he had a "proposition" for me: "The government of Pakistan owns the Roosevelt Hotel on East 45th Street. It is prime real estate but not considered one of New York's classiest hotels. It abuts Grand Central Station and controls the air rights to Grand Central. I have a deal for you about the Roosevelt property."

Trump said that he would like to enter into a fifty-fifty partnership with Pakistan, tear down the Roosevelt, and build "New York's finest mixed-used commercial, residential, condominium property, eighty stories tall, with the most commanding views of the city of New York."

The Roosevelt Hotel, named for President Theodore Roosevelt, was built in 1924. In 1974 Pakistan International Airlines (PIA), a subsidiary of the Government of Pakistan, leased the property with an option to buy it within twenty years. One of PIA's partners was Prince Faisal of Saudi Arabia. In 1989 the Roosevelt was valued at $140 million. (In 2007 PIA would put the Roosevelt on market for $1 billion. There were no takers. Pakistan still owns and operates the hotel to this day.)

I told Donald Trump that this kind of a commercial deal was not part of my portfolio of service to the government of Pakistan, but I would be glad to discuss the matter with him and inform the Prime Minister of his interest in a joint venture. But I questioned him about the nature of the partnership. I said that I was aware that the Roosevelt had been appraised at $140 million and that was considered a low estimate. Since he was talking about a fifty-fifty partnership, I asked what he was putting on the table.

He looked at me somewhat incredulously and said, "Come on Mark, you know what I'm putting into this deal; I'm putting in my name, that's what will make it a huge success."

I then spent the better part of two hours trying to explain to Donald Trump the nature of public sector representation. I told him that a fifty-fifty partnership with Pakistan putting in $140 million and him putting in his name might make sense as a business venture, but it would not make sense politically for the Bhutto government. I told him that any venture of this kind must be saleable to two hundred million Pakistanis, the Pakistani military and intelligence agencies, the Pakistani press, and the Pakistani political establishment. It not only had to be good business, it had to have good optics. It had to pass the smell test and the people of Pakistan would not understand a deal where they put up the money and he puts up his name. He kept arguing with me that this deal would make a fortune for Pakistan, and I kept answering that maybe it would, but it would bring down the Bhutto government because the terms he laid out were politically toxic.

It was pretty clear after a while that Trump was not getting my point about public sector representation, optics and smell tests, so I politely told him it was great meeting him and left his office.

I had no intention of communicating to the Prime Minister of Pakistan what Trump was proposing. I was not only Benazir's lobbyist and speechwriter, but I served as a political adviser as well, and what Trump was proposing could go nowhere. I thought the matter was done, but apparently it wasn't. I got another call from Trump's office ten days later saying that he would like to meet me again.

So, I flew back to New York thinking that Trump was going to make a counter-offer, possibly one that I could comfortably bring to the Prime Minister's attention. What I encountered was very different from what I expected.

First, Trump gave me an autographed copy of his book, *The Art of the Deal*, which was published in 1987. He had inscribed it to my son, writing, "To Bob Siegel, you have a great father, Best, Donald Trump." This was especially interesting to me because I had never told him that I had a son, and of course, never mentioned his name. But in any case, I thought this was pretty cool and thanked him.

We chatted for a few more minutes and then I said something like, "Donald, you wanted me to come back from Washington D.C. to meet again, so what's the deal?"

He immediately answered, "You know the deal."

He laid out the same fifty-fifty partnership that we originally discussed and that I had unambiguously rejected. There was no counteroffer, just more of his telling me how his name was going to make this a "huge, historic, unbelievable" success, and me telling him that it just wouldn't pass the optics test and it was something that I could never advise the Prime Minister to consider because it would be political suicide.

After a few minutes it was clear that we were going nowhere: he couldn't under-stand my concerns, and I obviously, as I had said before, couldn't accept the partnership he was proposing. I thought we were done and got up to leave. But we weren't done.

Donald Trump said, and I will never forget these words, "You know Mark, 'our building' is going to be the most fantastic building in New York, a building whose penthouses would have the greatest views of the city and would be worth millions. I bet Judy would love one of those penthouses."

It took me awhile to understand what Trump was saying. I had never mentioned my wife's name, but obviously he had done a bit of research. This man was essentially offering me a bribe. After a minute I told him that there just wasn't going to be a building on these terms and there were not going to be any penthouses. I again very politely thanked him for his time, got up, and left to return to Washington D.C.

Looking back on the incident, I realized that this maneuver was classic Trump, playing with other people's money, then in the end bullying and bribing. It was also classic in the sense that Trump seemed to have no comprehension or concern with the equities of public sector representation. He didn't care if a deal was right, as long as it made money, preferably without risking any of his own.

It also, in retrospect, demonstrated that Trump has limited concentration, could not understand issues that have a moral component, and just doesn't listen to people. Trying to educate or inform Donald Trump is a hopeless task. He demonstrated to me the qualities of human nature—or at least the darker qualities of human nature that would later define his presidency: arrogance, ignorance, corruption, indifference to norms and precedent, inability to learn, bullying, and greed. He was, and remains, purely transactional. He believes that the guiding principle of human nature is to acquire money or power at any cost. He lacks a moral compass or vocabulary.

Years later when we were making a speech in Venice, Italy, I retold the Trump-Roosevelt Hotel story to Benazir. She laughed, and said, "Really? Really? He said that? Really? 'Judy could have had a penthouse?'"

She laughed again. She told me I had done the right thing and I was right to cut it off before it ever got to her, because even considering such a proposition would have been politically harmful and embarrassing if it were found out. And, she said, "It couldn't have gone anywhere anyway." Then she laughed again and said with a wink, "Trump was dealing with the wrong man. The Pakistani press probably would say he should have talked to Asif" (her husband, who had a widespread but still legally unproven reputation for corruption and who was referred to by the hostile Pakistani press as "Mr. Ten Percent").

We both laughed together, never guessing that the man who attempted to bribe me somehow would become the forty-fifth president of the United States of America, still never learning or caring about political and moral optics and playing by his own set of rules—an international wrecking machine.

Me and bin Laden
Phil Noble

It was a few weeks after the 9/11 terrorist attacks and I was in my room at the Grand Hotel in Stockholm when the call came through. It was Crawford Cook, an old friend and the preeminent political and public affairs consultant in my home state of South Carolina.

As soon as I said hello, he launched into it with no introduction or explanation.

"I've got a really, *really* big favor to ask and you've got to do it," he said. I knew I was in trouble by the way he emphasized the second really.

First about Crawford. Crawford was a pro's pro. He was the first Democratic consultant in South Carolina who understood this new thing called television and how to use it in politics. As a result, he elected a string of governors, senators, and congressmen the likes of which haven't been seen before or since—Fritz Hollings, Bob McNair, and John West, among others.

When Jimmy Carter was elected president, he appointed his fellow governor John West to be ambassador to Saudi Arabia. Crawford went along for the ride and did a lot of work for the Saudi government. Crawford fit right in with the Saudi kings and princes as he was the very definition of extremely high-end, elegant perfection—in look, dress and manner. He was the first person I ever saw wearing a $5,000 custom-tailored suit. Charlie Cook, who knew Crawford at the time, claimed that Crawford had special boxes made to fit inside his suitcases so that he and his suits would arrive at their global destination without a wrinkle.

Crawford was near breathless when he launched into his pitch. "Over the years, Ambassador West and his law firm have been doing a lot of work with the bin Laden family and their global businesses. One of Osama's half-brothers, Yeslam, has agreed to do an interview with Diane Sawyer. And you've got to stop him and you are the only one who can do it," he said. Crawford obviously didn't know anyone else who was in Europe at the time and who was also fool enough to do it.

I knew from post-9/11 news reports that the bin Laden family had vast riches derived from their construction companies and other business amassed through their close relationships with the Saudi royal family. What I didn't know was who Yeslam bin Laden was, and I didn't know why I was the one to stop him from doing the interview.

Somehow Crawford had learned that I was in Europe and tracked me down. He wanted me to fly to Zurich where Yeslam lived and talk him out of the interview. As I tried to learn more and asked questions, Crawford kept getting more excited and finally he blurted out, "Phil you've got to go do this and you need to leave now for the airport as the next flight leaves in two hours."

"You've got to meet with him tomorrow morning as the interview is set for tomorrow afternoon," he said.

I was dumbfounded. He did convince me to get on the plane and he said he would fill me in on the details once I got to Zurich.

I said, "I'll get on the plane but I'm not committing to the meeting—and I'm damn sure not going to do it unless Ambassador West personally guarantees me that if it all blows up, he will hold a press conference and say that he asked me to do the meeting."

"Sure, sure," said Crawford, "just go get on the plane."

Ninety minutes later as the plane took off from Arlanda Airport, I had only one thought rattling around in my brain: what in the hell am I doing?

When I got to the hotel and called Crawford, the first words out of my mouth after his hello was, "I'm here in Zurich but I haven't agreed to the meeting or anything else."

There followed a nearly two-hour call, with a jumble of back and forth, and bits and pieces of information about Yeslam; his estranged wife and girlfriend, who were both publicly trash-talking him in the media about how he treated them; some big-time business deals that were all going south; something about a new line of luxury fragrances Yeslam wanted to promote—and all sorts of other disjointed things.

As we finished the call, Crawford gave me Yeslam's office address and said that he was expecting me at nine a.m. I repeated that I hadn't agreed to do anything and I'd think about it overnight.

I didn't sleep much.

The next morning at 8:45, I found myself still undecided trying to walk inconspicuously along the street in front of Yeslam' s compound—all the while looking for spooks with guns from the CIA, Mossad, al Qaeda, or God knows who else on rooftops and in the bushes.

I decided to do it.

Just as I was walking up the path to the entrance, a low-flying helicopter buzzed me overhead. "That's it," I thought as I was sure that within a few seconds my picture was going to be flashed onto the computer screens of spy agencies all over the world.

I walked into the compound, was shown to a large elegant office, and ushered into a beautiful antique chair in front of a big gold Louis XIV desk. I figured the chair cost more than my annual income and I could probably have retired on the price of the desk.

Soon a short, compact man walked into the room. He greeted me very properly and I was served strong, sweet Arabic coffee. With a minimum of small talk, he began telling me about how he wanted to do the interview to repair his family's image, protect his business empire, restore better relations between the U.S. and Saudi Arabia—and on and on. He said how he had talked to Diane Sawyer several times. She had assured him that she would be even-handed and let him get his story across.

After fifteen minutes or so, he stopped talking and asked, "Do you think I should do the interview?"

I looked him straight in the eye and explained that I was there as a favor to Ambassador West; I was not getting paid and I didn't want to get paid. I was there to simply give him my best professional opinion.

"For twenty-five years, I have been a political consultant working in over forty states and a dozen foreign countries," I began. "In all those years, this is the single dumbest idea I have ever heard—nothing else even comes close."

I told him how Sawyer was one of the most skilled, cut-throat interviewers in all the world and about how within five minutes she would butcher him like a newborn lamb based on what his wife and girlfriend said about him. Then she would put him through a fine meat grinder until he was just as a mass of kibbeh nayyeh (an Arabic raw ground lamb dish). Then she would ridicule and humiliate him about the 'bin Laden fragrance'—all this before she even got to Osama and September 11.

He was taken aback as he was not used to people talking to him like this. He sat silently. When I finished, he looked down for a full five minutes without saying a word.

He then looked up and said, "I won't do the interview."

Having completed my task, I stood up. He walked over to me, took my hand, and with near tears in his eyes said, "You have kept me from making a big mistake. If there is ever anything I can do for you, please ask me."

I thanked him and walked out. I've never seen or talked to him since.

I got back to the hotel, called Crawford and told him what happen.

"Thank God," he exclaimed.

"Now," I replied with an attitude, "you and Ambassador West owe me a really, really big one."

He agreed. Unfortunately, they have both passed on without my ever collecting— but at least I did get a damn good story out of it.

Ed Koch
Victor Kovner

In the 1988 Democratic presidential primary election, we were supporting U.S. Senator Al Gore. New City Mayor Ed Koch wanted to endorse Gore. We had nothing going on in the state; we had nothing to lose. The next day, Al had a press conference announcing Koch's endorsement. Ed used the whole press conference just to attack Jesse Jackson. And we watched it on television and you could see Gore moving out of the picture to be off the screen. He was embarrassed by Koch's behavior.

Koch was always totally self-centered. It was always about him.

Bella Abzug
Sarah Kovner

Bella Abzug was a congresswoman from New York City. She was a very outspoken feminist and civil rights advocate. When I say outspoken, she seemed very loud and to many people, abrasive—but not to us. That's how she came across.

She and Ed Koch did not see eye-to-eye. They hated each other. Their styles were different. He was so focused on himself. Issues didn't really matter to him. At one point, they ended up living in the same building, Two Fifth Avenue. Occasionally, they would meet in the lobby and have a conversation. Both out of office, their careers were over, and they were older and more mellow.

Bella dies. After the funeral, there was a shiva (Jewish week-long mourning for the deceased) in her apartment and I was there—I was working for Secretary of Health and Human Services Donna Shalala in Washington D.C. I went down to the lobby to wait for Donna. I'm in the lobby and Ed Koch comes in. He saw me and he said, "I'd like to go up to Bella's apartment, but I don't know if I would be welcome. Would you find out?"

Bella would've welcomed him, but her daughters and family, and the women's Strike for Peace people would be there. So, I went up and I asked if they would receive him nicely and they said yes. Then he came up just to pay his respects.

It was his final goodbye.

Eleanor Roosevelt

Sarah Kovner

We decided to organize a group of activist women by having a ten a.m. meeting—after kids were off to school. We ask Eleanor Roosevelt to come and meet with this group of women. We were upstairs waiting when we realized it was a fifth-floor walk-up apartment. It had never occurred to us we were asking Mrs. Roosevelt to walk up five flights of stairs. She was in her seventies. She seemed older because she had been the First Lady for four terms and U.S. Ambassador to the United Nations.

Of course, there was nothing we could do about it. Women were already upstairs. We went down to meet her and apologize. But she said, "It's fine."

She walked up upstairs, and she said, "When Franklin was running for the legislature in Poughkeepsie in Duchess County, the Democrats always lived on the top floor."

Robert Morgenthau

Victor Kovner

My first real campaign experience occurred when I was working for former New York Governor and U.S. Senator Herbert Lehman and his candidate for governor, Robert Morgenthau. Bob Morgenthau wasn't yet forty. He had served with distinction in the Navy during the war, but he hadn't really done much.

Lehman got him that nomination. I'll never forget—I went with him up to the state convention in Syracuse that year. Bob was a terrible candidate, the worst. He was shy beyond words. We had rallies for him, but you couldn't find him. He was a wonderful person with fine values, but as a candidate, what a joke. Republican Nelson Rockefeller won by a landslide.

Later, Morgenthau was Manhattan District Attorney when Judge Sonia Sotomayor was up for nomination for the U.S. Supreme Court. A judicial appointment panel existed to review appointments, including Democrats and Republicans. Bob Morgenthau was one of the panelists. He was revered—even by the Republicans.

The Republicans were giving her a hard time because she was a member of the Puerto Rican Legal Defense Fund. A Republican asks a member of a panel, "Well, isn't it questionable that a lawyer should be on a group with, you know, such ethnic, partisan commitments?"

Morgenthau said, "I insist that all my assistants join such groups, like the NAACP Defense Fund, the Puerto Rican Legal Defense Fund—it's a must in my office."

That was the end of that conversation

Knowing John Glenn
Dale Butland

When I served as U.S. Senator Glenn's press secretary, I became one of John's closest aides—and often traveled with him either alone or with his wife, Annie. Often that meant flying co-pilot with him in his twin-engine Beech Baron that he regularly flew back and forth between Ohio and Washington, D.C. When I flew with John, he'd have me sitting co-pilot with him and I'd have the ear sets on, and he'd have me twist dials, do this and that. I still to this day have no idea what the hell I was doing. No idea.

I've also never been crazy about flying in small planes. But as I used to tell my wife, "If you have to fly on a small plane, you can do worse than have John Glenn as your pilot." Nevertheless, I resigned myself to the reality that if that plane had ever gone down, I wouldn't have been mentioned until the fourth or fifth paragraph: "Also on board. . .."

It was during those flights that John would often tell me stories I never heard him tell anywhere else—-including one that I included in the op-ed I wrote for the *New York Times* when the Senator passed away in December of 2016.

The story was about Bobby Kennedy, with whom John had become close after his orbital flight as an astronaut in 1962. They were about the same age and just hit it off really, really well. President Kennedy was not somebody John could pal around with, but he did with Bobby. And they got so close that their families would some-times vacation together, like on a camping trip down the Snake River in Idaho.

By 1968, John had retired from the Marine Corps and taken a job as president of Royal Crown International, where he also served as vice president for the parent company. He told me, "It was just life-changing. We were living in New York and they were paying me $100,000 a year, which at that time was real money."

"For the first time in our lives, Annie and I didn't have to worry about putting our kids through college or taking care of our parents as they got older.

"Things were going great for us. Then that spring, Bob (John never called him "Bobby," it was always "Bob") decides to run for president in 1968. He asked if I'd campaign for him and I told him I would.

"A few weeks later, I'm at home—-and I get word that there's going to be an emergency meeting at the Royal Crown board the next day.

"So, a guy calls me, one of my friends on the board, and says, 'John, I want you to know this meeting is aimed at you.'"

"What do you mean?" John asked him.

The fellow said, "Well, the purpose of the meeting is to pass a resolution saying that no member of the Royal Crown board can be involved in partisan politics in 1968. Turns out the powers that be aren't real crazy about having one of their highest profile executives linked to Bobby Kennedy."

"Next day comes, we walk into the meeting in the company's board room. When everyone was seated, but before the chair of the board started the meeting, I stood up and said 'It's my understanding the purpose of this meeting is to pass a resolution saying that no member of the Royal Crown board can be involved in politics in 1968. But I want everyone to know that Bob Kennedy has asked me to campaign for him and I told him I would. And I will because he's my friend. And if that means we can't continue our association together anymore, I can live with that. But I want you all to understand what's going to happen if that occurs. We're going to walk out of this meeting. You're going to hold your press conference and I'm going hold mine. We'll see who comes out better.'"

John continued, "There was some coughing and people looking down at their shoes. And then the chairman finally just gaveled the meeting over without the resolution ever coming up."

I think this story is a window into the kind of person John was. He was willing to sacrifice the first financial security his family had ever known to keep a promise to a friend.

Zero G's and Feeling Fine

Dan Mowbray

The first time I met U.S. Senator John Glenn, I was directing him in a TV commercial. He was endorsing a candidate for mayor of Columbus, Ohio. And why not? The candidate, Dr. John Rosemond, had served as navigator-bombardier in WWII with the famed Tuskegee Airmen. If I had only known! I would have loved to have heard Rosemond and Glenn discuss their flying experiences.

I learned my lesson that day. Know your subject, always have a question ready, and look for the opportunity to learn something along the way.

In the intervening years, I had various other occasions to work with the astronaut turned senator. My production company even put together a full-size replica of his Mercury spacecraft for a tribute that featured then Vice President Gore. On every occasion I filmed him, Glenn was everything one would want a hero to be: unfailingly cooperative, courteous, and fighter-pilot punctual.

So, imagine my panic one foggy morning years later when I pulled into the parking lot of John Glenn High School in New Concord, Ohio, and found John and Annie Glenn waiting on their own, with my film crew nowhere in sight. As I silently cursed the crew, my stomach sank. But the Glenns couldn't have been nicer and graciously invited me to wait in the back seat of their car.

How cool is this? I thought as we climbed in.

The crew finally showed up and while we were waiting for the setup, I played for time. It happened I'd just read a couple books, one about Glenn and another about Douglas MacArthur. I asked whether Glenn, who'd had served in the Pacific during the Second World War, had ever met General MacArthur.

"Only once," he said.

"Annie and I were in New York, staying at the Waldorf-Astoria, where MacArthur had a suite. We had just finished a parade when we received a phone call. The general would like to meet us. Would Annie and I and the kids come up? So, we went up, and there we were, sitting the four of us on a couch when MacArthur came in. There was a big wing-backed chair in front of us. He sat down in it and surveyed us, while we, dressed in our Sunday best, stared back. Then he addressed us as if he was addressing Congress."

Naturally, I pictured the scene. The Glenns—a Norman Rockwell family if ever there was one—Glenn with his Marine style haircut and bow tie, Annie and the kids—wide eyed, facing the imposing and stern-looking General of the Army.

Glenn, an extremely pleasant man, but not inclined to joking around, bust into a full-bore imitation of MacArthur, in a deep and sonorous voice. "This is the greatest day in the history of the cosmos!" he intoned, with all the "MacArthurian" grandeur.

Glenn's words, quoting MacArthur, stick with me to this day—they were so unusual and over the top. But to anyone who'd heard MacArthur's farewell to Congress—"Old soldiers never die, the just fade away"—Glenn's parody rang true. The general was a ham, even when addressing a young family from New Concord.

By the way. . .did you know that Charles Lindbergh flew beside John Glenn during World War II in the Pacific? I didn't either until I heard about it the other day on the CBS show, Sunday Morning. I'll bet John Glenn had a million stories like that which he never thought anyone would be interested in. . .unless, of course, some asked. Luckily, I did.

Our household treasures include an autographed picture of Glenn, the famous one on the cover of Life magazine. Yet what is more memorable to me was how human Glenn was in that unplanned, unscripted moment. I cherish the memory of that day, when an extraordinary man showed his lighter side, he and his wife being nice as they could be to a nervous young man.

Too Funny to Run
Robert Neuman

The distinction between Morris Udall and the rest of the sizable field seeking the 1976 Democratic presidential nomination was his relentless use of humor. In fact, after a Milwaukee press conference aimed to hit hard at U.S. Senator Scoop Jackson's hawkish record, he left the prepared remarks to tell the following story.

Jackson, not known for his humor, attempted to tell a joke during this campaign. The joke involved the newly sworn-in President Gerald Ford meeting with the newly resigned Richard Nixon. Nixon stumbled and bumped into Ford and said, "Pardon me, Jerry!" Ford replied, "Dick, I already did."

When Jackson attempted to tell the joke, he had Nixon stumbling into Ford and saying, "Excuse me Dick!" So much for the punch line. The media attending the conference roared and the planned attack on the "Hawk" Jackson was derailed.

Commentator Robert Novak wrote that "Udall was primed to attack Jackson, a task to which he is spectacularly unsuited," and columnist James J. Kilpatrick concluded, "The fact is Mo Udall is too funny to be president." That resulted in the title of Mo's book on political humor published in 1988.

I am reminded when the *Wall Street Journal's* John Pierson questioned Mo's qualifications to serve in the highest office in the land: "Mo, you have a great record as a legislator, speaker, and even a writer, but are you prick enough to be president?"

Mo was stunned by the question. After a pause, he said, "I don't really know." Then he recounted his narrow loss in a race to be House Majority Leader. "I know the difference between a cactus and a caucus—a caucus has the pricks on the inside."

The line that best fits his 1976 campaign was later uttered by the *Washington Post's* David Broder, "Mo Udall wanted to run for the White House in the worst way. . . and he did!"

I Don't Know If I Have Alzheimer's or Not
Garry South

In 2002, I was running California Governor Gray Davis's re-election campaign. Davis's numbers were underwater due to the electricity crisis and blackouts in 2000 and 2001. President George W. Bush's strategist Karl Rove, sensing a weakened Davis, recruited former Los Angeles Mayor Richard Riordan, a supposedly moderate Republican, into the Republican primary, thinking he was the best candidate to beat Davis in the fall.

We also decided Riordan would be our toughest general election opponent. So, we decided to spend $10 million trying to take Riordan out in the GOP primary—a risky move that worked, with Riordan sliding from a forty-one-point lead over the eventual primary winner to eventually losing to him by eighteen points.

Our intervention was described in *the New York Times* as a "political hall of fame move." Riordan never forgave me. At the end of the primary, when his eventual defeat became pretty obvious, Riordan held a press conference at the greasy-spoon restaurant he owned in downtown Los Angeles, and thundered, "Garry South is a bad man! Garry South is a bad man!" (His private security goons barred me from the conference, but I could hear his shouting clear out on the sidewalk.)

I had actually thought, though, that we had developed at least a decent working relationship by 2004, as I got both him and State Controller Steve Westly to co-chair the "Yes on Proposition 62" campaign that I was running that year, which would have installed a top-two primary system in California. By 2006, I was the chief strategist for the gubernatorial campaign of Westly in the Democratic primary. Toward the end of the primary, I had one of the most bizarre and yet funny conversations I had ever had with a politician.

Riordan called me on my cell phone and the conversation went like this:

ME: "Hello, Mr. Mayor."

RIORDAN: "You answer this question I'm going to ask you, and if you answer it honestly, I won't sue your ass!"

ME: "Excuse me?"

RIORDAN: "You told the *Los Angeles Times* I have Alzheimer's!"

ME: "Huh, I have no idea what you're talking about. How would I know if you have Alzheimer's? Plus, it may surprise you, but I don't really think about you much anymore."

RIORDAN: "You're lying, someone told me they heard you said it. I'm going to sue your ass for libel!"

ME: "Wait, someone told you they heard me tell the *Los Angeles Times* you have Alzheimer's?"

RIORDAN: "No, someone heard you tell someone else you told the *Times* I have Alzheimer's."

ME: "Oh, so now you're down to third-party hearsay. You're supposed to be a crack lawyer, shouldn't you know that won't stand up in court, Dick? Also, as a lawyer, shouldn't you be threatening to sue me for slander, not libel, since what you claim I said never ended up in print?"

RIORDAN: "I want you to take a lie detector test. I'll take one, too."

ME: "Oh, don't be ridiculous, I have no intention of taking a lie detector test, but you can go ahead and take one, though."

Then, out of nowhere in this heated conversation:

RIORDAN: "I don't know if I have Alzheimer's or not. I've never taken the test."
ME: "Bye, Dick."
He never called me back and didn't sue me.

As Grave a Thing as Any
Jim Guy Tucker

I was once quoted in a newspaper story as saying that I ultimately got comfortable with the death penalty. What I thought I had told the reporter was I was a little different than most of the other Arkansas governors who had faced the death penalty issue.

After the U.S. Supreme Court struck down the death penalty in 1972, Governor Winthrop Rockefeller pardoned everyone on death row before he left office. So, when Governor Dale Bumpers took over, he had no one on death row, and his successor, Governor David Pryor, faced the same situation. It wasn't until Governor Bill Clinton that a governor had to deal with the issue. And I had something to do with that as well.

When I served as state Attorney General in the 1970s, we created a new criminal code and I re-wrote the death penalty statute. In order to have the death penalty, first a jury had to decide if a defendant was guilty or not guilty, and then the jury had to consider aggravating and mitigating circumstances. Prosecution would put on aggravating circumstances and the defense put on mitigating. In this proceeding, the defendant could testify because, having been found guilty, the defendant was not going to put him or herself in jeopardy. Finally, the jury had to find that the aggravating circumstances outweigh the mitigating circumstances before the death penalty could be issued. We got rid of the death penalty for rape—it was just for murder. In 1976, the U.S. Supreme Court allowed the death penalty under limited circumstances and the Arkansas statute was upheld.

So I have been through all of the legal issues associated with the death penalty as Attorney General.

Also, death was something I'd confronted most of my life. I'd known I had an autoimmune disease since I was in college and I knew that my own life would likely be a short ride. I had been in Vietnam twice. I had been in intense battles and I had seen an awful lot of people killed, both enemy soldiers and American soldiers. As a prosecutor, I'd seen horrible crime scenes. I watched my father, mother, and sister die. For these reasons, and religious reasons as well, death does not carry the fear and horror for me that it does perhaps for others.

But I do fear the misuse of governmental power. I saw it from the time I was in high school with integration, when a governor totally disregarded the law, human rights, and the U.S. Constitution in order to keep children from going to school together because of their race.

And I am deeply concerned about the horror of racial disparities in the criminal justice system. To this day, I've been testifying before the legislature and working with a committee at the law school trying to eliminate racial disparities in sentencing that arise frequently from social factors.

You take something as profound as death and combine it with the power of the government, and there's no question that there needs to be extraordinary care taken. When I served as governor of Arkansas, I took the executions very seriously. I had absolutely superior attorneys on my staff. I got a report from my folks, I read the transcripts, I sat up in bed at night, and I spent huge amounts of time on every case.

Once a person asked to meet with me and asked me not to put a family member to death. The convicted defendant had murdered a Black state trooper down in southwest Arkansas, but was then acquitted by an all-white jury in a white county.

One of the guns the police found had been involved in the killing of a Jewish pawn-shop keeper. The defendant was sentenced to death for that. He was not a young man and he was not a young man when he committed the crimes.

Then the state police asked me two nights before his execution not to carry it out, to defer it and stop it for the time being. I asked, "Why are you asking me to do this?" They finally told me there had been multiple threats made against me and that the convicted defendant was associated with a group that was very, very dangerous. It was the same group that was linked to the Oklahoma City bombing.

I absolutely refused. I said, "We're not stopping anything because someone is threatening the governor of the state. That's not going to happen." And it didn't. I thought the jury's verdict was correct. There was overwhelming evidence of guilt in the case.

The case that I'm puzzled on, and it troubled me a great deal, was of three men who were convicted at the same time for the same crime. Years before they had escaped from penitentiary together. They then burglarized a house and stole at least one weapon with ammunition. The state police surrounded them shortly afterwards at a different location. As it happened, a Black state policeman walked out unarmed to try to talk them into surrendering. One of them killed him while he was standing there trying to ask them to give up. It was horrible because they were young when they committed the crime and this was years later.

So, I had to deal with three executions on the same night. And three executions at one time was really, really hard—hard on my staff, hard on the prison staff, hard on my wife, and hard on me.

An execution is as grave a thing as any that a government can do.

Speechless
Jerry Austin

After Bill Clinton was elected president in 1992, his Lt. Governor, Jim Guy Tucker, became governor of Arkansas.

My firm, Austin Sheinkopf, was hired to produce the media for his election campaign in 1994. I was chosen to be the point person mainly because of my success in electing and re-electing a governor in Ohio—Richard Celeste.

Sometimes in a campaign you're lucky. You hit it off with the candidate. That's exactly what happened.

Governor Tucker was a client who became a friend. I not only liked Jim Guy, I liked his wife Betty as well. They were a team. She was his closest adviser.

On a typical election night, with many clients with races that day, I would stay at home monitoring election results. Not this election night in 1994. The governor invited my wife and I to join him, his family and friends, at his watch party. We accepted even though we knew he was going to have a huge victory. He won by twenty points.

During the campaign, I had visited the governor's mansion but never stayed overnight in the guest house. It was important to separate politics from governing.

After the campaign, I kept in touch with the governor via phone, and when I was in Little Rock on other business, I'd stop by his office to check in.

One day, he called me and asked if I could come to Little Rock to have dinner with him, on a specific night, and to stay at the guest house in the mansion. I, of course, replied yes. I had no idea the reason for this invite.

I arrived for dinner and soon realized the governor and I were the only two having dinner. No Betty; no kids.

He told me the reason he asked me to come was to keep him company that evening because triple executions were scheduled to take place. He did not want to be alone.

I was speechless.

I asked why he chose me? He said he knew I could carry on an interesting conversation and I had experience being with a governor during trying times.

After dinner, we spent the next few hours talking about politics and life—but not death. He kept looking at his watch. At the time the act was to take place, he looked at the phone, waiting for the official notification the executions had taken place.

I retired to the guest house and left the next day.

Another *True Tale from the Campaign Trail*—and a unique one.

About the Contributors

Gerald (Jerry) Austin has been one of the nation's most experienced and successful political strategists. Austin has consulted on races throughout the United States at every level from precinct committee person to president of the United States. Raised in the Bronx, Austin learned his politics in Cleveland in the late 1960s. After helping elect Richard Celeste Governor of Ohio twice, he became the campaign manager for Reverend Jesse Jackson's 1988 presidential campaign. He was the senior political director for Paul Tsongas's 1992 campaign for president and helped elect Paul Wellstone to the United States Senate. In 1992, he was the consultant and media adviser for Carol Mosely Braun's historic campaign for the U.S. Senate. His work also includes witnessing the Marcos/Aquino election in the Philippines; the Pinochet plebiscite in Chile; and many trips to Northern Ireland to consult for the SDLP party. Austin earned a B.A. in American History from the City College of New York; a Master's in Public Administration from New York University; and a Master's in Education from The University of Akron. He served as an Adjunct Professor and Director of the International Campaign Fellows program at The Bliss Institute of Applied Politics at The University of Akron.

Tom Beres was the senior political correspondent for WKYC Channel3, the NBC affiliate in Cleveland, Ohio for thirty-seven years before retiring in 2016.

Over his career, he won four Emmys, two for investigative reporting, and was inducted into the Cleveland Press Club Hall of Fame.

Dale Butland is the president of Butland & Associates, a politics and media relations consulting firm. He the former chief of staff and press secretary for U.S. Senator John Glenn, serving from 1980 to 1999.

Jack Corrigan is an attorney and Democratic Party consultant. He rose to prominence within the party when he served as a senior member of Governor Michael Dukakis' 1988 campaign for President. Corrigan served as convention manager for the 2004 Democratic National Convention in Boston, where he selected Illinois State Senator Barack Obama to give the keynote address.

Evan Dobelle was elected mayor of Pittsfield, Massachusetts in 1973 and 1975, and later served as Massachusetts State Commissioner of Environmental Management and Natural Resources. He was the treasurer of the Democratic National Committee and National Chairman of the Carter-Mondale Presidential Committee, and was U.S. Chief of Protocol for the White House during the Carter administration.

Tony Fazio is the founder of the direct mail firm Winning Directions. He has over forty years of experience working on hundreds of campaigns in the political communications industry, including candidates, labor organizations and issue campaigns all across America.

Bill Fletcher is CEO and partner of Fletcher Ridge & Co. He is a writer, photographer, musician, and film and video director. He has worked on hundreds of political and corporate campaigns across the US and internationally. Bill excels in strategic communications and the production of high-quality multimedia projects.

Terry Fleming is a retired lobbyist who formerly served as executive director of the Ohio Petroleum Council and worked at the Ohio Chamber of Commerce.

Les Francis served as Rep. Norman Mineta's first congressional chief of staff before moving to Jimmy Carter's White House as deputy assistant to the president and eventually deputy White House chief of staff. He remained active in national politics and public affairs from offices in Washington, D.C., for four decades before returning to his native California in 2016.

David Heller is one of the top political media consultants and campaign strategists in the Democratic Party. As president of Main Street Communications, an award-winning political media firm, Dave has compiled the best won-loss record in the Democratic Party, helping clients win election to Congress.

Sarah Kovner, a longtime activist and candidate adviser, Kovner served as a founding board member of the Coalition for Free Choice, the National Women's Political Caucus and the First Women's Bank of New York. She became the President of Arts, Letters and Politics, a public affairs consulting firm serving a wide range of non-profit organizations. She then served as the Special Assistant to the Secretary of the Department of Health and Human Services throughout the Clinton administrations. Kovner is also a member of the Democratic National Committee.

Victor Kovner is a Democratic activist and a partner at David Wright Tremaine LLP. Mr. Kovner represents national and regional broadcast and print media clients in all aspects of communications law, in addition to his work in intellectual property and commercial litigation. He has served as Corporation Counsel of the City of New York (the City's chief legal officer) and is also a founder of J Street, a nationwide organization that seeks to advance a two-state solution for Israel and Palestine.

Kitty Kurth, the President of Kurth Lampe Worldwide, is a public relations and political strategist with Chicago know-how and global reach. She has worked on the last eight American presidential campaigns in roles of press secretary, campaign manager, and communications adviser, and every four years works with speakers at the Democratic National Convention.

Celinda Lake is a leading political strategist, serving as tactician and senior adviser. Celinda is president of Lake Research Partners, which is known for cutting-edge research on issues including the economy, health care, the environment, and education. Her international work has included work in Liberia, Kyrgyzstan, Belarus, Ukraine, South Africa, and Central America.

Kevin Lampe is a co-founder of Kurth Lampe Worldwide. In his career, he has worked on campaigns from U.S. President to local school boards. Lampe has served in senior roles in several American presidential campaigns, directing media relations and outreach, campaign strategy and messaging, media/debate preparation and training.

Joanne Limbach is a specialist in state and local state policy, serving as tax commissioner for the State of Ohio Department of Taxation and member of the cabinet of Governor Richard F. Celeste. She is past president of the Federation of Tax Administrators and a former director of government affairs for The Success Group, Inc.

Dan Mowbray is a retired independent broadcast media professional who previously wrote for the *Columbus Dispatch*.

Robert Neuman was former Press Secretary and close friend of Congressman Mo Udall. In 1974 he joined Udall's congressional staff and worked on his 1976 campaign for the Democratic nomination for president. He then became communications director of the Democratic National Committee in 1979 and served there until 1984 when he rejoined Mo Udall as Chief of Staff. He is now retired living in Annapolis, Maryland.

Phil Noble is recognized globally as one of the leading experts on uses of the Internet in the civic sector—in politics, media, government, and public affairs. In

1996, Noble founded PoliticsOnline, the premier international company providing news, tools, and strategies for the civic sector globally. Noble was a Democratic candidate for Lieutenant Governor of South Carolina in 1994 and was a Democratic candidate for Governor of South Carolina in 2018.

Katherine Rogers is a Democratic Party member of the New Hampshire House of Representatives, having served from 2012 to 2020 and 1992 to 1998, and previously in various local offices. She has extensive experience in campaigns across the country.

Steve Rosenthal is an American labor and political strategist. Rosenthal served for seven years as the political director of the AFL-CIO, stepping down in August 2002. At the time, *The New York Times* reported that many union leaders credited Rosenthal with "transforming organized labor's feeble, forgettable campaign operation into one that many political analysts say is the most effective in the nation."

Sal Russo is the founder of Russo Marsh + Associates, Inc. (RMA) and has spent over fifty years in the field of political consulting, advertising, and public affairs. Mr. Russo began his political career as a special assistant to Governor Ronald Reagan after serving in his 1966 gubernatorial campaign, and later became Deputy Chief of Staff to Governor George Deukmejian's after managing is 1982 gubernatorial campaign. In 2009 he co-founded the Tea Party Express, which has become one of the largest grassroots conservative political action committees in the nation.

Hank Sheinkopf is president of Sheinkopf Communications, a full-service strategic communications company serving corporate, political and public affairs clients. He has worked on an estimated seven hundred political campaigns on four continents, in fourteen foreign nations and forty-four American states over the last thirty-five years. His political clients have included President William Jefferson Clinton, New York City Mayor Michael Bloomberg, Leonel Fernandez, former President of the Dominican Republic, and former President of Mexico, Vicente Fox.

Mark Siegel is a Democratic Party activist and White House official. He was executive director of the Democratic National Committee under the chairmanship of Robert S. Strauss, the first Jewish chairman of a major American political party (1973–77). Siegel became deputy assistant to President Jimmy Carter in January 1977, where he served as the liaison to the American Jewish community. For more than twenty years after leaving the White House, Siegel served as president of Mark A. Siegel and Associates, Inc., and International Public Strategies, Inc., lobbying firms dealing with domestic and international representation.

Rick Silver formed Chernoff/Silver & Associates in 1976 after serving as an aide for two lieutenant governors. Since then, his ideas have gotten bigger and better in a wide variety of fields—from education, healthcare, and economic development to energy, the environment, and insurance. Rick's reputation precedes him as an expert in research methodology and analysis, opinion polling, issues management, and public relations.

Garry South, principal of the Garry South Group, has nearly forty years of experience at high levels in government, politics, and business consulting. Garry has worked for both the federal government and state governments in three different states and has managed or played leading roles in numerous campaigns. He served as Midwest Regional Finance Director of the Democratic National Committee and is a specialist in the political use of radio.

Curt Steiner is CEO of Steiner Public Relations and is well known in business, government, media, and higher education circles. Steiner leads his high-performance communications and public affairs firm with vast experience in media strategy, press relations, communications, politics, reputation management, lobbying, campaign management, corporate consulting, and government policy-making.

Raymond Strother is called the "consultant's consultant" by his peers. Universities teaching campaign management named him "a living legend in 2003." He was a Resident Fellow of the Institute of Politics at Harvard, a member of the Journalism

Hall of Fame at LSU, and an Honorary Fellow at The University of Akron Bliss Institute of Applied Politics. He is a past president of the American Association of Political Consultants and has been inducted into the Gulf Coast Museum for his lifetime contribution to campaigns.

William Sweeney was the president and chief executive officer of the International Foundation for Electoral Systems (IFES) from 2009–2018. He served as deputy chairman of the National Democratic Committee, executive director of the Democratic Congressional Campaign Committee, and part of the management team for seven U.S. presidential inaugurations.

Donald R. Sweitzer is one of The Campaign Group's founders and is a veteran of two presidential campaigns. Doc has successfully elected more than thirty members of Congress and statewide elected officials. He brings a special expertise in media targeting and is a regular guest lecturer across the country on political strategy and media planning.

J. Warren Tompkins has had an enduring impact on South Carolina politics for nearly three decades. Highly regarded as a shrewd political strategist, his advice has been sought throughout the Southeast in local, state, and national races. At First Tuesday Strategies, Warren has acted as a head consultant to various state and local level campaigns.

Jim Guy Tucker served as the forty-third Governor of Arkansas, 1992 to 1996, after serving as the fifteenth lieutenant governor, 1977 to 1979, and the forty-ninth attorney general, 1873 to 1977.

Gerry Tyson is president of the Tyson Organization in the Dallas/Fort Worth area. After spending more than a decade with another firm, Gerry Tyson founded The Tyson Organization in 1983 and has since served Democratic and progressive clients in fifty states, planning and executing telephone-based programs for campaigns at the local, state and federal levels.

Tom Vilsack served as the fortieth governor of Iowa from 1999 to 2007 and as United States Secretary of Agriculture from January 2009 until January 2017, returning to this position in 2021.

Jack Walsh owns Jack Walsh and Associates, whose clients include Dukakis for Governor 1974, Massachusetts League of Cities, Massachusetts Selectman's Association, and the Massachusetts Mayors Association. He has worked as campaign manager for Mayor White's bid for governor, Director of Field Organization in Dukakis for Governor, and an adviser to Congressman Thomas O'Neill, Jr.'s campaigns for Congress.

Mark Weaver is the founder of Communications Counsel, a crisis communications expert with three decades of experience advising clients in twenty-five states and at the highest levels of national government and major corporations. He served as the Deputy Attorney General of Ohio, and on the Attorney General's Executive Staff as a senior policy adviser and chief spokesman.

Joe Slade White was president and founder of Joe Slade White & Company. In 2014, White was named "National Democratic Strategist of the Year" by the American Association of Political Consultants. White's past clients have included presidential candidates, U.S. Senators, governors, members of Congress and mayors as well as statewide and local initiatives throughout the country. He passed away in 2021.

Printed in the United States
by Baker & Taylor Publisher Services